First Stage

MW01703378

Copyright © 1985 by Kathy Henderson

All rights reserved. No part of this book may be reproduced or utilized in any form or by any means, electronic or mechanical, including photocopying, recording or by any information storage and retrieval system, without permission in writing from the Publisher. Inquiries should be addressed to Permissions Department, William Morrow and Company, Inc., 105 Madison Ave., New York, N.Y. 10016.

Library of Congress Cataloging in Publication Data

Henderson, Kathy, 1954–
First stage.

Includes index.
1. Actors—United States—Biography. I. Title.
PN2285.H4 1985 792′.028′0922 [B] 85-6522
ISBN 0-688-04700-9 (pbk.)

Printed in the United States of America

First Quill Edition

1 2 3 4 5 6 7 8 9 10

BOOK DESIGN BY LINEY LI

For Ken and for my mother

Preface

One of the fringe benefits of regular theatergoing is that you become a great amateur talent scout. I, for example, discovered Kevin Bacon in 1980 in *Album,* Glenn Close in *The Crucifer of Blood* (1978), Kevin Kline in *On the Twentieth Century* (1978), John Shea in *Sorrows of Stephen* (1979), and Meryl Streep in *The Cherry Orchard* (1977). As America's moviegoers got to know them, I felt a little smug. After all, I saw them first.

It's nothing new, of course, for talented performers to move from stage to screen. What *is* new is the continuing loyalty of so many terrific young actors to the stage—and their commitment to dual careers rather than the single-minded pursuit of "stardom." It's a trend that makes me optimistic about the future of both theater and film in this country.

The photographs assembled here attest to the tremendous range of roles undertaken by twenty of my favorite actors. I picked these particular people because their work has given me a lot of pleasure and also because I feel that they really care about what they do. (In any profession these days, that quality is rare.) An arbitrary age limit of forty helped me keep the list down, as did the strict rule that each of them actually started out on the stage. Though I talked with almost all of them and with some thirty of their colleagues, I can't tell you what they are "really like." I can show you what they've done, though, and that's what's important.

Acknowledgments

I'd like to thank the actors in *First Stage* for their generosity in talking with me about their work. I'm grateful as well to the producers and directors who shared their insights and to the theatrical photographers represented in the book.

Four special people deserve particular thanks for their help and support: Deborah Kletter of Triad Artists, Catherine Olim of PMK Public Relations, Martha Swope (a wonderful photographer and fellow cat lover), and William Treusch. Thanks also to Lisa Bailey, Phyllis Carlyle, Jim Curtain, Diana Dussant, Susan Geller, Chris Karatnytsky and the entire staff of the Billy Rose Theater Collection/New York Public Library at Lincoln Center, Richard Kornberg, the staffs of Phototeque and Cinemabilia, Sheila Robinson, Carol Rosegg, Richard Sims, Betsy Sofisberg, Arnold Stiefel, and the research staff at the Television Information Office.

For their cooperation and consideration, thanks to Columbia Pictures, MGM/UA Entertainment Company, Orion Pictures Corporation, Paramount Pictures Corporation, Showtime, Tri-Star Pictures, Twentieth Century-Fox Film Corporation, Universal Pictures, and Warner Bros. Inc.

Finally, I want to say thanks to my supportive editors, Kristina Lindbergh and Alison Brown Cerier, and to colleagues who gave me special assistance: Jan Cherubin, Nina Combs (for the title), Roger Director, Shea Fantel, Cathi Hanauer, Ellen Kunes, Karen Larson, and Patrick Pacheco.

Contents

Kevin Bacon

"When I was seventeen or eighteen, what I really, really wanted was *Footloose,*" says Kevin Bacon. "That was my dream—to explode in a movie and to be on the cover of magazines. Now that it's happened, although it's been great, other things are more important."

Coming from Bacon, those words don't sound like false modesty or cynicism. Eight years in New York have taught him a lot about success. "I've had enough tastes of it to develop a certain perspective," he notes.

His first taste came at nineteen, a year after he'd moved to New York from his hometown of Philadelphia. Like most aspiring actors, Bacon had spent the year as a busboy, waiter, and acting student. After a casting director for *Animal House* stopped by Circle in the Square Theatre, where Bacon was studying, the preppy-looking young actor found himself playing a haughty Omega fraternity pledge in what was to be the first and funniest youth comedy film. (A rampaging crowd literally flattened him at the end of the movie.) Thinking he was on the fast track to stardom, Bacon immediately got an agent—and ended up waiting tables again for a year.

An interesting choice then came up: to take either a supporting role in the spinoff TV series *Delta House* or a nine-line part in Marsha Norman's Off-Broadway drama *Getting Out.* He chose the play. "The series just didn't feel right to me, though it certainly meant more money than I had ever seen," he says. "The play sounded exciting, and I was starting to enter a theatrical circle. I just knew that New York was where I wanted to be."

A year later, he was rewarded with a lead role in *Album,* David Rimmer's comedy about coming of age in the sixties. As a cocky yet vulnerable high-school hero, he helped turn the play into a

"KEVIN BACON SKILLFULLY STEERS BILLY FROM HIS BABY JOCK EGOTISM TOWARD A CONFUSED CONSERVATISM."

—MARILYN STASIO,
New York Post

With Keith Gordon, Jenny Wright, and Jan Leslie Harding in Album *(1980), Cherry Lane Theatre, New York*

Gary Wheeler/Equity Library Theatre

With Randall Robbins in Glad Tidings *(1977), Equity Library Theatre, New York*

"KEVIN BACON MOST EFFECTIVELY CONVEYS THE CONFUSION OF THE ACTRESS'S SON, WHO WOULD RATHER LEAD A NORMAL LIFE THAN RUN ALL OVER THE WORLD IN THE SHADOW OF HIS MOTHER."

—ALVIN KLEIN,
New York Theatre Review

Animal House *(1978)*

surprise Off-Broadway hit. "Kevin brought so much to the rehearsal process," recalls director Joan Micklin Silver, "investigating not only his own character but his relationship to the others. He's extraordinarily talented and inventive."

At the same time, Bacon was playing a teenage alcoholic in the daytime soap opera *The Guiding Light.* "It's not something I would want to do again," he says of soap work, "but it enabled me to live in the city and work on the stage. The show was respectful of my nighttime career."

Bacon went on to win Obie awards for playing a street hustler in *Forty-Deuce,* Alan Bowne's graphic depiction of homosexual prostitution in Times Square, and a Yale Whiffenpoof member in *Poor Little Lambs* (1982). He also received good reviews for his 1982 Off-Broadway work as a troubled student in *Flux* at the Second Stage.

On the big screen, he'd been murdered while making love in

Friday the 13th (1980) and did a pick-up scene with Kristy McNichol in *Only When I Laugh* (1981), but Bacon got his first real chance to shine in *Diner* (1982). Sneering the correct answers to the *G.E. College Bowl,* shooting the breeze with his friends, drunkenly climbing into the manger of a nativity scene, he more than held his own among the film's talented newcomers.

A star is born? Not yet. "I was still struggling to prove that I could do a lead," he says. "My character in *Diner* was dark and troubled, and people get very nervous about 'Can he carry a film?' All this metaphysical bull about presence and magnetism—it has nothing to do with being an actor. Stage directors and producers have a lot more imagination." Rather than play a string of uninteresting "friend" roles, he endured another siege of unemployment.

Then a stage role got things moving once again. "If you're in a play," observes Bacon, "you're very hot. After opening night, you're going to have scripts flying at you." *Slab Boys,* a drama about

"KEVIN BACON EXCELS AT SUGGESTING AN AMBIVALENT MIXTURE OF SUSPICION, ADORATION, AND EXASPERATION, AND HIS ULTIMATE EXPLOSION AT HIS INSTRUCTOR TERRIFIES THE AUDIENCE AS WELL AS THE CHARACTERS."

—TISH DACE,
Other Stages

Copyright © 1982 Stephanie Saia

With Robyn Goodman in Flux *(1982), Second Stage, New York*

Copyright © 1984 Martha Swope Associates/Carol Rosegg

"THOUGH THE GIFTED MR. BACON IS NOT IDEALLY CAST AS AN ASPIRING WORKING-CLASS HERO, HE USUALLY CAPTURES THE CONFUSED PHIL'S MIXTURE OF YEARNING, SELF-PITY, AND RAGE."

—FRANK RICH,
The New York Times

With Sean Penn in Slab Boys *(1983), Playhouse Theatre, New York*

young workers in a Welsh carpet factory, limped through a two-month Broadway run in the spring of 1983, but Bacon and co-star Sean Penn generated a good deal of heat. "I had a great time," says Bacon, "but it was the hardest part I ever played. It never really gelled all the way for me."

One of the scripts he read during the *Slab Boys* run was *Footloose,* which became an honest-to-goodness eighty-million-dollar box-office hit. Yet Kevin Bacon almost wasn't in it.

"The studio didn't think I was good-looking enough," he says. "So I went through makeup tests, hair tests—it was the 'Is he handsome?' screen test." Through it all director Herbert Ross insisted that Bacon could indeed bring something special to *Footloose.*

"I had seen Kevin in *Diner* and *Slab Boys,*" he says, "and I thought he was a terrific actor with a lot of dimensions. The part [in *Footloose*] was very underwritten, and I felt he had a quality that would enrich it—an interesting internal life. He's a very serious and intelligent person."

The movie centers around the lead character's efforts to bring dancing back to a conservative midwestern town, but Ross wasn't deterred by Bacon's lack of dance training. "He was musical," the director says, "and he was willing to work hard. I also thought the role rested more on his ability to deliver the acting scenes." Testing completed, Kevin Bacon won the part—and later on, the magazine covers he'd once wanted.

"THE GIFTED OFF-BROADWAY ACTOR KEVIN BACON GIVES [FENWICK] A SELF-MOCKINGLY SATANIC LAUGH AND DISSOLUTE GOOD LOOKS—HE'S BOTH ATTRACTIVE AND CREEPILY SELF-DESTRUCTIVE."

—DAVID DENBY,
New York

Copyright © 1982 Metro-Goldwyn-Mayer Film Co. and SLM Entertainment, Ltd.

With Mickey Rourke, Daniel Stern, and Timothy Daly in Diner *(1982)*

More important, *Footloose* helped him make the jump to his first adult lead, in an adventure film called *Quicksilver,* filmed in the fall of 1984. But Bacon expects to continue working onstage and to keep home base in the east. "I live mostly in the country now," he says, "and I've been able to buffer myself against the 'Hollywood life-style.' My life hasn't changed that much." He'd have to admit, though, that he's come a long way from busing tables.

With Lori Singer in Footloose *(1984)*

"KEVIN BACON AS REN IS A SMASHINGLY CREATIVE, CHARMING, AND MAGNETIC ACTOR WITH AN ENORMOUS RANGE."

—REX REED,
New York Post

Copyright Theo Westenberger/Liaison

Matthew Broderick

A handsome actor in his early twenties might be expected to cash in on his first hit movie by doing several more teen-oriented films as quickly as possible. Not Matthew Broderick. In the two years after the hoopla of *WarGames,* he made a big-budget ($21 million) medieval adventure called *Ladyhawke,* then a tiny-budget ($1.6 million) family drama called *1918.* The rest of his time was devoted to *Brighton Beach Memoirs,* the Broadway hit that earned him a 1983 Tony Award, its sequel, *Biloxi Blues,* and a cable-TV production of Athol Fugard's play *Master Harold . . . and the Boys.*

Broderick is too down-to-earth to classify himself as a serious actor—he's at a loss even trying to explain how he chooses roles—but his directors find his maturity impressive. Gene Saks, director of both *Brighton Beach* and *Biloxi Blues,* calls him "one of those young people who's really beyond his years—there's an original mind there."

"He's very careful about what he does," adds John Badham, the director of *WarGames.* "He's not being pushed into doing anything just to generate income. He has to like it and believe in it."

The twenty-three-year-old actor grew up in a family that fully understood the demands of a theatrical career: mother Patricia, now an artist, was a writer and director; father James, who died of cancer in 1982, was a respected stage actor and star of the TV series *Family.* By the time Matthew entered Manhattan's Walden School, he was interested in performing, though his parents never pushed him either way.

"I used to love the whole atmosphere of theaters," says Broderick, who spent many summers traveling the straw-hat circuit with his father. "The nervous energy backstage, where everybody has to be real quiet, the bright lights onstage once the curtain goes up—it's very special."

"MR. BRODERICK IS EVEN MORE APPEALING HERE THAN IN HIS LAST APPEARANCE AS EUGENE. . . . HIS COMIC TIMING, NOW AS MUCH PHYSICAL AS VERBAL, HAS ATTAINED A TEXTBOOK PERFECTION."

—Frank Rich,
The New York Times

With Randall Edwards in Biloxi Blues *(1985), Neil Simon Theater, New York*

Copyright © 1984 Ken Howard

With Harvey Fierstein and Estelle Getty in Torch Song Trilogy *(1981), Richard Allen Center for Cultural Art, New York*

"TEENAGER MATTHEW BRODERICK GIVES ONE OF THE MOST ORIGINAL, WITTY, AND TOUCHING PERFORMANCES I'VE EVER SEEN FROM A YOUNG ACTOR."

—JACK KROLL, *Newsweek*

Father and son acted together only once, in a workshop production of Horton Foote's *Valentine's Day,* just before Matthew finished high school in 1979. "I was very nervous," he recalls. "There were scenes where he had to scream at me in this weird Southern accent and I found it hard to take it seriously. It always felt like Dad pretending to be an old Southerner."

Soon after graduation, Broderick won the lead role in a film called *No Small Affair* opposite Sally Field. He was understandably ecstatic—until the picture shut down after two weeks when director Martin Ritt became ill. (It was finally made several years later with other actors.) "That was awful," he says. "It took me almost two years to get another job."

When he did get a job, it didn't seem like much at first. He'd be playing a gay teenager in the third act of a four-hour-long play in a tiny theater for practically no money. Against his agent's advice, Broderick took the part and thus became an original cast member of *Torch Song Trilogy* in 1981. His work won critical praise and led to his being cast in both a Neil Simon movie (*Max Dugan Returns*) and play (*Brighton Beach Memoirs*).

"IT'S TO THE GREAT CREDIT OF EVERYONE RESPONSIBLE FOR *MAX DUGAN RETURNS*—MR. SIMON, MR. ROSS, MISS MASON, MR. BRODERICK . . . THAT THE FILM REALLY FLIES. IT'S WELL ACTED, SPEEDILY PACED, AND FULL OF OUTLANDISH SURPRISES."

—Janet Maslin,
The New York Times

Copyright © 1983 Twentieth Century-Fox Film Corp.

With Marsha Mason in Max Dugan Returns *(1983)*

Brighton Beach Memoirs *(1983), Alvin Theater, New York*

"THE VERY HEART OF THE PIECE IS EUGENE, THE 15-YEAR-OLD SON WHO SERVES AS NARRATOR AND CENTRAL CHARACTER. HE IS GIVEN A KNOCKOUT PERFORMANCE BY MATTHEW BRODERICK. PLAYING A PESKY ADOLESCENT WHO SEEMS TO RECOIL AND ADVANCE AT THE SAME TIME, HIS FRAME CURVED IN AND HELD BACK EVEN AS HIS WORDS LEAP FORWARD WITH NASAL INSISTENCE, HE IS BOTH HILARIOUS AND WINNING."

—Douglas Watt,
New York *Daily News*

In the charming though little-seen *Max Dugan,* Broderick and Marsha Mason play a son and his mother forced to cope with extravagant gifts proffered by Mason's long-lost father (Jason Robards). Already Broderick's gift for sly, almost self-mocking comedy was in evidence.

Before starting rehearsals for *Brighton Beach,* he was tapped to star in *WarGames* as a computer whiz who almost starts World War III. "Virtually everybody under the age of twenty was tested for the role," says John Badham. "Matthew has a nice, easy quality and a remarkable sense of comedy and timing. He was quite good at driving his scenes forward with a sense of humor."

By the time *WarGames* became one of the biggest hits of 1983, Broderick had won Broadway's Tony for *Brighton Beach Memoirs.* He was funny, charming, and believable as a Depression-era teenager in Neil Simon's autobiographical play.

"Matthew is actually a wonderful character actor," says Badham. "Most young actors can really only play themselves well, but the character in *Brighton Beach Memoirs* is very different from the one in *WarGames.* He has a nice chameleon quality."

Broderick's next three projects demonstrated the truth of that statement. First, he traveled to Italy to play a wily thief nicknamed "the Mouse" in *Ladyhawke.* His character manages to escape from a dungeon prison, then agrees to help break the spell separating two thirteenth-century lovers. (The film was actually made eighteen months before its April 1985 release.)

Next, he gave a splendid performance as a troubled South African teenager in *Master Harold . . . and the Boys* for the Showtime cable network. Broderick had strong memories of two other Fugard plays he had seen as a child, and the TV production allowed him to work with Tony Award–winning actors Zakes Mokae and John Kani.

In the film *1918,* he portrayed an older version of the same Southern character he had played onstage with his father in *Valentine's Day.* Horton Foote's screenplay, based on his own childhood, explored the events of the year in a small Texas town stricken by a flu epidemic.

Then it was back to the stage in Neil Simon's *Biloxi Blues,* Broderick's first chance to play a character on the verge of adulthood. "It's also a romantic lead in a way, which I haven't had a chance to do," he says. "Anyway, there's a girl in it and also a hooker, so I finally get to lose my virginity." Again, the critics marveled at the charm and poignancy of his performance.

For Matthew Broderick, the choice to combine theater and film work seems natural. "Plays are what first attracted me to acting," he points out. "I really like doing both stage and movie work, and I wouldn't want to do without either."

"YOUNG MATTHEW BRODERICK, A TONY NOMINEE FOR HIS CURRENT BROADWAY PERFORMANCE IN NEIL SIMON'S *BRIGHTON BEACH MEMOIRS,* IS VERY SERIOUS AND GRAVE—AND THUS VERY APPEALING—AS THE UNASSUMING COMPUTER WIZARD."

—VINCENT CANBY,
The New York Times

Copyright © 1983 United Artists Corporation

With Ally Sheedy in WarGames *(1983)*

C. David Batalsky/Showtime

With John Kani and Zakes Mokae in Master Harold . . . and the Boys *(1984), Showtime (cable TV)/PBS*

"BRODERICK SHINES AS HAROLD. HE LETS NOTHING—NEITHER HIS ACTING NOR THE SOUTH AFRICAN ACCENT HE TAKES ON SO EFFORTLESSLY—UPSTAGE THE SCRIPT. BRODERICK MAY STILL LOOK LIKE A TEEN STAR, BUT HE IS A MATURE ACTOR."

—JEFF JARVIS,
People

Glenn Close

Glenn Close's Tony and Obie awards, and her nominations for three Oscars, an Emmy, and another Tony, reflect her ability to bring to life an array of characters with little visible effort. Though she's known to movie audiences for a series of selfless Earth Mother roles (in *The World According to Garp, The Big Chill,* and *The Natural*), Close has done everything from musicals to Restoration comedy on the New York stage.

"I like a good story and a good acting job," she says, "and in that way, I find there's not much difference between theater and film. The thing that's frustrating about movies is that you always think you could have done something better. When you're lucky enough to be in a hit play, you have the luxury of constantly trying something new. It's a wonderful ongoing process with your fellow actors and with each audience."

Raised in Greenwich, Connecticut, Close began performing in a repertory group called the Fingernails ("the group with polish") while attending the Rosemary Hall school, and played Romeo during her senior year. She delayed entering college to tour the country with folk-singing groups in the late sixties, graduating from the College of William & Mary's drama department in 1974 at age twenty-seven.

After taking part in special student auditions sponsored by the Theater Communications Group, Close was accepted into New York's Phoenix Theater Company. Within weeks, she got the break all understudies dream of. The play was Congreve's *Love for Love,* and director Harold Prince remembers opening day very clearly:

"I had been waiting for weeks for [lead actress] Mary Ure to learn her lines. She implied to me that she was what we call a 'money player'—that she'd be there by opening night. On Broadway, there are three or four openings and we got through

"GLENN CLOSE GIVES AN EXQUISITELY SENSITIVE PERFORMANCE AS ALBERT NOBBS, WHO AWAKENS IN ALL TRAGIC INNOCENCE TO THE EMOTIONAL BARRENNESS OF HER LIFE AS AN OBSESSIVELY EFFICIENT WAITER IN A DUBLIN HOTEL."

—Marilyn Stasio, *New York Post*

The Singular Life of Albert Nobbs *(1982), Manhattan Theatre Club, New York*

Copyright Van Williams

Love for Love *(1974), Helen Hayes Theater, New York.*

"MISS CLOSE IS A TOUCHING ACTRESS, AND HER WARNING HINTS OF LOVE THROUGHOUT THE PLAY, A BLUSH ON A ROSE PETAL, WERE ADMIRABLY DONE."

—CLIVE BARNES,
The New York Times

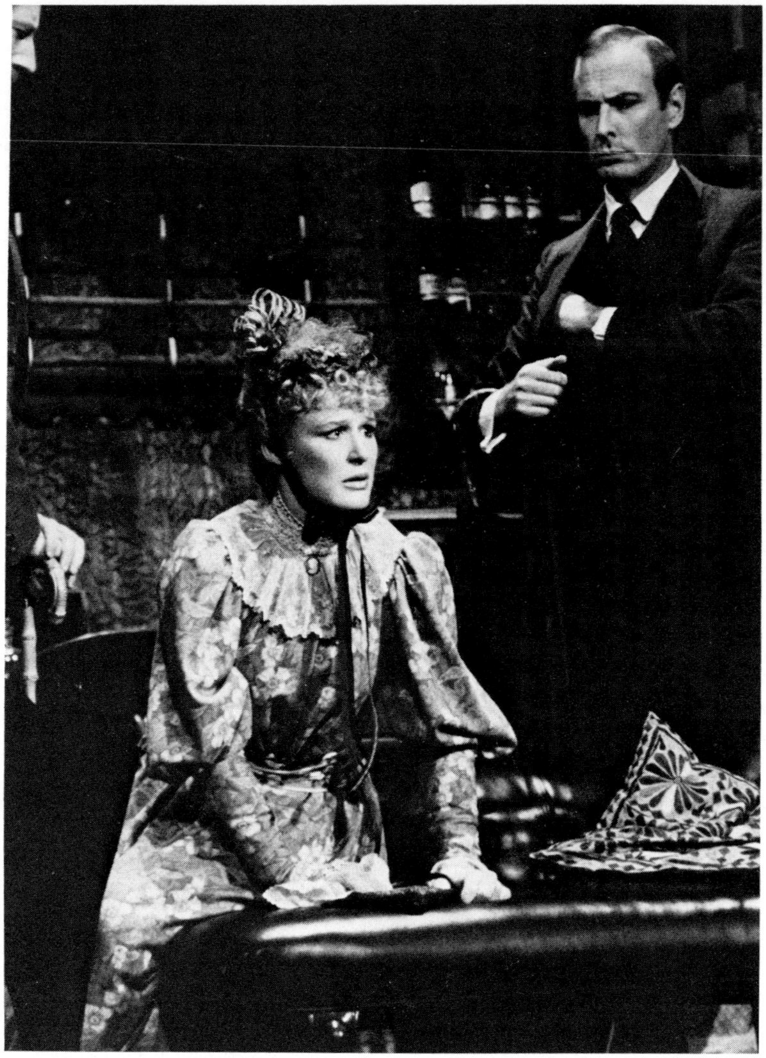

Copyright © 1984 Martha Swope

With Paxton Whitehead in The Crucifer of Blood *(1978), Helen Hayes Theater, New York*

"GLENN CLOSE AS THE HEROINE OF THE ADVENTURE RUNS HER GAMUT STRONGLY FROM DISTRAUGHT TO REGAL. THE WHOLE BLOODY THING IS STYLISHLY DONE."

—JULIUS NOVICK,
The Village Voice

the first one, but again she let the company down. I'd been watching Glenn Close, and I thought she could do it. So I went backstage at five o'clock in the afternoon and said to Glenn, 'Do you think you can go on?' She said yes. We worked for two hours on her scenes. I then stepped in front of the curtain and told the audience that this night, they would be seeing someone who had joined Equity two weeks earlier. She went on, and she was just fine."

During the next few years, Close appeared in regional theater productions of *A Streetcar Named Desire, King Lear,* and *The Rose Tattoo,* as well as in a flop Broadway musical (*Rex,* 1976) and a hit Broadway play (*The Crucifer of Blood,* 1978). Her first Tony

Copyright © 1984 Martha Swope

With Jim Dale in Barnum *(1980), St. James Theatre, New York*

"GLENN CLOSE IS A SPLENDID MRS. BARNUM, WITH THE AMBIGUITIES OF A PASSIONATE PURITAN ETCHED INTO THE WILY, PINCHED PRETTINESS OF HER FACE, HER VERY PRESENCE EXUDING THE SOUR-SWEET JOYS OF CIRCUS LEMONADE."

—JOHN SIMON, *New York*

nomination came in 1980 for *Barnum,* a musical that proved to be her entrée into feature films.

Barnum was developed as a showpiece for the multitalented Jim Dale, but Close won her share of praise as his feisty wife, Charity. Still, it wasn't her singing or dancing that caught film director George Roy Hill's attention—it was her serene presence as she sat alone in a box onstage before the play began.

"She had a stillness about her that I thought was remarkable," Hill recalls. "I wanted to have that quiet assurance in my film." The movie in question was *The World According to Garp,* and Glenn Close gave a powerful performance as Garp's mother, the efficient, imperturbable nurse Jenny Fields. Her work earned an Oscar

Copyright Jean Pierre Laffont/Sygma

The World According to Garp *(1982)*

"AS GARP'S MOTHER, THE LUST-HATING, INDOMITABLY WILLFUL NURSE JENNY FIELDS, GLENN CLOSE STRIKES A NEAR PERFECT BALANCE OF YANKEE FORTITUDE AND MONOMANICAL COMMON SENSE. SOMEHOW, SHE MAKES THIS MONSTER MADONNA HUMAN."

—DAVID ANSEN,
Newsweek

nomination and admiring notices from critics who wondered where this unknown actress had come from.

Close returned to the stage even before *Garp* was released in a fact-based Off-Broadway drama called *The Singular Life of Albert Nobbs.* She received unanimous praise and an Obie for playing a Victorian woman who pretends to be a man in order to find work.

Her second film, *The Big Chill,* was a memorable ensemble effort and a surprise hit. As Sarah, the sensible wife who urges husband Kevin Kline to father a baby for their friend (Mary Kay Place), Close became the movie's emotional hub and picked up another Academy Award nomination.

Next, she co-starred with two of America's foremost actors: Robert Duvall in *The Stone Boy,* a drama about the death of a child, and Robert Redford in *The Natural,* a mythical tale about baseball and the power of dreams. (As Redford's childhood sweetheart, Close received her third Oscar nomination.) Both films added to her ethereal image, as did *Something About Amelia,* an ABC-TV movie about incest. *Amelia,* which aired in January 1984, drew sixty million viewers and earned Close an Emmy nomination. The Emmy ended up going to Jane Fonda and the 1984 Oscar to Linda Hunt, but Close won the 1984 Best Actress Tony for Tom Stoppard's *The Real Thing.*

Given the chance at last to portray a sexy, headstrong woman

Copyright © 1983 Columbia Pictures Industries, Inc.

The Big Chill *(1983)*

"GLENN CLOSE, AS KEVIN KLINE'S WIFE . . . POSITIVELY GLOWS WITH GENEROSITY AND NURTURING WARMTH."

—David Denby, *New York*

in Stoppard's dazzling play, Close attacked the role of Annie, Jeremy Irons's actress wife, with gusto. So believable was the chemistry between them that unfounded rumors popped up of a real-life romance.

Her six-month run in *The Real Thing* reinforced Close's love for stage acting. "Even if a role is difficult, there's something thrilling about it when you come to a night and you fly," she says. "The variables are different every time you go into the theater. To me, that's deeply exciting."

"IF ANNIE CAN BE A THANKLESS ROLE, THE FRIZZILY RED-HEADED MISS CLOSE CONCEDES NOTHING. SHE'S WARM AND PERSUASIVE EVEN WHEN HER CHARACTER'S CONVICTIONS AND BEHAVIOR ARE DUBIOUS. MORE IMPORTANT, SHE JOINS WITH HER CO-STAR TO GIVE THE PLAY ITS ESSENTIAL SEXUAL CHARGE."

—FRANK RICH,
The New York Times

Copyright © 1984 Martha Swope

With Jeremy Irons in The Real Thing *(1984), Plymouth Theatre, New York*

Once again, a film director found himself inspired by Close's stage performance. "Glenn has an incandescent beauty and the ability to really lose herself in a character," says Paul Aaron. Immediately after seeing her in *The Real Thing,* he asked her to play the lead in *Maxie,* a movie that promises to put an end to her being typecast as a nurturer. In this fall 1985 release, Close plays a secretary possessed by the ghost of a flamboyant silent-screen actress. It's a sexy, funny part, and Close is well matched with co-star Mandy Patinkin.

"Glenn works miraculously well on film because she acts so with her eyes," says Aaron. "I knew that if she chose to do a comedy, letting it all out would be great fun for both of us. It requires tremendous ability to play two different characters without benefit of gimmick or funny makeup."

Close calls *Maxie* "the hardest thing I've ever tried to do. I played a character who would intimidate me if I met her. Sometimes I'd go into a scene and think, 'I can't do this.' But you just have to throw yourself out there and *do it.*"

Copyright © 1985 Orion Pictures Corporation

With Mandy Patinkin in Maxie *(1985)*

Lindsay Crouse

Lindsay Crouse is physically small, but her crystalline voice and natural poise command attention. "She has a simplicity and dignity that endow her characters with a remarkable translucence," says Marshall Mason, who has directed her in *Hamlet, A Streetcar Named Desire,* and other plays. "On film," he notes, "we are accustomed to being in close and seeing the stillness of the human being and therefore understanding what is going on inside. But when someone is as rooted and grounded on the stage as Lindsay is, it's an extraordinary thing to behold."

As befits a well-trained actor who happens to be the daughter of one famous playwright (Russel Crouse), the namesake of another (Howard Lindsay), and the wife of a third (David Mamet), Lindsay Crouse discusses acting with an emphasis on the spoken word.

"To really grow, an actor needs to deal with language," she says firmly, "because the analysis of the text in order to learn how to play a scene is, as far as I'm concerned, the art of acting. There's no better place to practice that than on the stage. In a film, the content really comes in a cut—two pictures are juxtaposed and then the viewer puts together the meaning. In the theater, *we* supply that transition; *we're* the editors. For me, it's never a question of going back to the stage; it's a question of going away from the stage in the first place."

Crouse grew up surrounded by her father's glittering circle of theatrical colleagues and friends. After graduating from Radcliffe in 1970, she briefly considered a career as a modern dancer. Unsure of her commitment, she turned to acting and spent the next five years studying and performing Off-Broadway and at regional theaters. In New York, her first real showcase was *The Foursome* (1973), a battle-of-the-sexes drama; at the Kennedy Center in

"AN OUTSTANDING SHAKESPEAREAN PERFORMANCE. . . . [CROUSE] IS A BEACON OF LOVELINESS AS THE WILLFUL VIOLA. WHILE PRETENDING TO BE BOYISH, SHE MAGICALLY RETAINS A FEMININE RADIANCE. SHE WOULD BE PERFECTLY SUITED TO PLAY ALL OF SHAKESPEARE'S GIRL-BOY ROLES, AND WOMANLY CHARACTERS AS WELL."

—Mel Gussow, *The New York Times*

Twelfth Night *(1980), Circle Repertory Company, New York*

Washington, D.C., she had small parts in *Present Laughter* (1975) and *Long Day's Journey into Night* (1976). She broke into movies as a reporter in *All the President's Men* (1976), followed by larger roles as an underground newspaper photographer in *Between the Lines* (1977) and the drunken wife of a hockey player in *Slap Shot* (1977).

In 1979, Crouse began a fruitful two-year stint with Marshall Mason's Off-Broadway Circle Repertory Company. "Circle Rep was a lifesaver for me," she says. "I was going around and around in the big centrifuge of regional theaters, and I was trying to come

With Timothy Meyers, Carole Monferdini, and Matthew Cowles in The Foursome *(1973), Astor Place Theatre, New York*

Copyright Kenn Duncan

"IN THE FEMALE LEAD, LINDSAY CROUSE CREATES A SOARING PORTRAIT OF SPOILED SOUTHWESTERN FEMALE ESSENCE. CATCHING THE MERCURIAL MOODS OF THIS CAGED ANIMAL, SHE SAUNTERS, CRAWLS, AND PETULANTLY SQUEALS HER WAY ACROSS ELWIN TERRELL II'S LOVELY CHUNK OF BEACH WITH A CHARGED AND APPEALING THEATRICALITY."

—DICK BRUKENFELD, *The Village Voice*

home [and work in New York]. The thing that's so difficult about the acting profession in the United States is that you can't get any traction. Without those Circle Rep productions, I would still be floating around the regional theaters. Marshall was one of the first people who simply believed in me."

Crouse's Circle Rep performances as Ophelia in *Hamlet* and Viola in *Twelfth Night* won raves, and she picked up an Obie Award for her work in her husband's trio of one-act plays, *Reunion* (the former two productions were staged by Mamet as well).

"I love having David direct me," Crouse says. "His strength as a director is his strength as a human being—he's an absolute purist. That can be tremendously frustrating at times. You just want to scream, 'I'm human! Go away and leave me alone!' But if you can stand up to each other and work as colleagues, it's very strengthening for the marriage. The hardest thing about it is that you can't seem to leave your work at the theater."

"LINDSAY CROUSE AS THE FRUSTRATED WIFE OF A MYSTERIOUSLY IDEALISTIC PRINCETON ALUMNUS ON THE TEAM IS ALLOWED TO GLOW AND GROW IN A PART THAT MAKES LITTLE SENSE AS WRITTEN."

—Andrew Sarris, *The Village Voice*

Courtesy of Universal Pictures

With Paul Newman in Slap Shot *(1977)*

Copyright © 1984 Gerry Goodstein

With Michael Higgins in Dark Pony (Reunion) (1979), Circle Repertory Company, New York

"MISS CROUSE AND MR. HIGGINS ARE IDEAL FOR [MAMET'S] PURPOSE—AND FOR ANYONE ELSE'S, I'D THINK."

—EDITH OLIVER, *The New Yorker*

"IT IS LINDSAY CROUSE WHO GETS RIGHT TO THE HEART OF THE MATTER WITH THE MOST PENETRATING OPHELIA IN MEMORY."

—DOUGLAS WATT, New York *Daily News*

With William Hurt in Hamlet *(1979), Circle Repertory Company, New York*

Mamet says he tries "to emulate the examples of charity, intelligence, and honor which she, in her daily life, sets [for] me—and I had better not upset her or I will never be allowed to go to sleep."

In addition to Mamet and Marshall Mason, Crouse cites Sidney Lumet as an especially supportive influence in her career. She has appeared in three Lumet films: as an Italian wife in *Prince of the City,* an Irish nurse in *The Verdict,* and a Jewish Marxist in *Daniel.* The director calls her "one of the only young actresses I know who has strength without having to reach for it."

Copyright Barbara Walz/Outline

The Verdict *(1982)*

"LINDSAY CROUSE HAS ONLY A FEW MINUTES ON CAMERA AS THE KEY WITNESS IN THE CASE, BUT SHE MAKES THE MOST OF THEM."

—KATHLEEN CARROLL,
New York *Daily News*

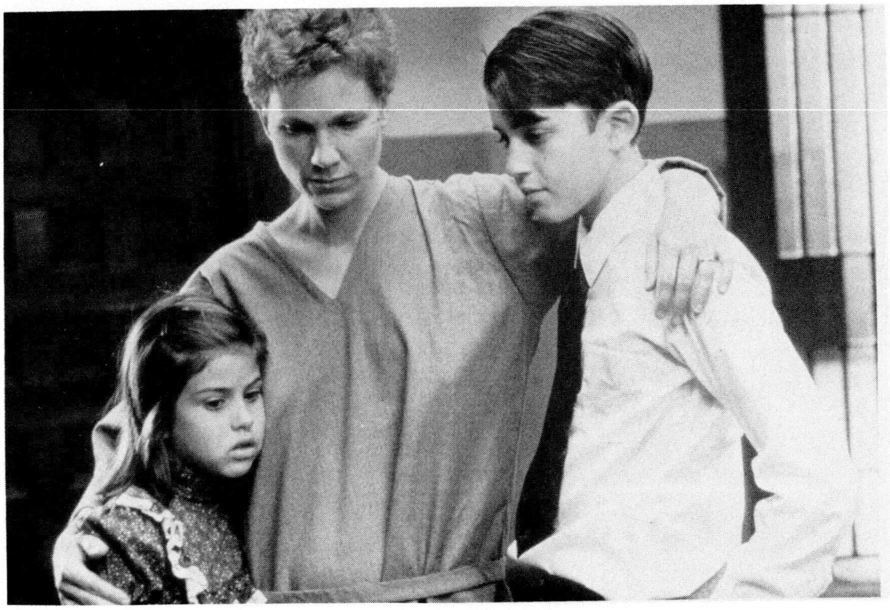

Copyright © Liaison

With Jena Greca and Ilan M. Mitchell Smith in Daniel *(1983)*

"I DON'T KNOW WHAT LINDSAY CROUSE IS PLAYING—[E. L.] DOCTOROW DOESN'T CREATE CHARACTERS, HE HAS HIS OWN PATENTED CUTOUTS—BUT SHE PLAYS WELL. SHE'S A FLESH-AND-BLOOD PRESENCE, AND SHE'S CONVINCING AS A POLITICALLY INVOLVED WOMAN OF HER TIME."

—PAULINE KAEL,
The New Yorker

Places in the Heart *(1984)*

To Crouse, there's a lesson in the enthusiastic response she received for her role as key witness in *The Verdict.* "That movie really put me on some kind of map, and it was wonderful, but I had to constantly remind myself that it was *one very short scene,*" she says. "It's illusory, this world of Hollywood that would snap you up on the basis of a scene and say, 'Your work is wonderful.' You have to be very clear with yourself that that doesn't make you an experienced actor. We don't have theater stars anymore, so you tend to drink it up when someone finally says to you, 'That was a great job.' The kinds of response you can get from a movie performance are out of proportion to the work that was done."

Given those reservations, Crouse says she finds film acting "exciting and rewarding—it's the hundred-yard dash." Most recently she played a scientist in *Iceman* and brought her special dignity to the role of Sally Field's sister in Robert Benton's *Places in the Heart,* winning a 1985 Oscar nomination.

"CROUSE MAINTAINS A COOL DIGNITY AS THE SISTER WHO ONLY BECOMES AWARE OF HER HUSBAND'S LOVE AFFAIR WITH HER BEST FRIEND WHEN SHE NOTICES THE SCHOOLTEACHER SUDDENLY WITHDRAW HER HAND FROM THE HUSBAND'S GRASP."

—KATHLEEN CARROLL,
New York *Daily News*

"Lindsay has a wonderful sense of herself," says Benton, adding that he'd wanted to work with her since seeing her performance in *Slap Shot.* "When we were rehearsing her big scene with Ed Harris, all of a sudden it was like the battleship *Missouri* had sailed into the room with all guns blazing. She blew everybody away. From that moment on, the quality of rehearsal just went up and up. She is terrific."

Crouse longs to act in Shakespeare or to play her favorite role, Stella in *Streetcar,* on Broadway. Oddly enough, her only Broadway appearance was as an extra in *Much Ado About Nothing* in 1972. "Broadway is no longer a place to do plays," she says, citing the high cost of productions and ever-rising ticket prices. Discussing her plans to star in Mamet's new translation of *The Cherry Orchard* in Chicago, she says, "Nobody would back that on Broadway—the first thing they'd say is to put it in a three-hundred-seat theater. We've got wonderful contemporary playwrights, too, but a certain grass-roots kind of theater is getting lost. We just have to keep going, perhaps try to make a new theater if we can.

"I want to be a very fine actor," she goes on, "and whatever the economics of the country I live in, I've just got to find the best places to keep working. Acting is always so difficult. You never quite feel that you've solved the mystery of it. But I feel more and more that I know what my job is."

"THOUGH MISS CROUSE MUST DEFINE THE ONE UNDERWRITTEN ROLE BY SHEER WILL, [SHE DOES] RISE TO TOP (AND AT TIMES FUNNY) FORM."

—FRANK RICH, *The New York Times*

Copyright © 1984 Stephanie Saia

With Dianne Wiest, Peter Weller, and Jimmie Ray Weeks in Serenading Louie *(1984), Second Stage, New York*

Gregory Hines

Gregory Hines creates instant excitement with his feet. When he taps, people don't just listen, they cheer in amazement at an artistry that appears absolutely effortless.

"Gregory is a great dancer and a great performer—he knows how to sell his wares," says tap choreographer Henry LeTang, who began teaching Hines and his older brother Maurice more than thirty-five years ago, when Gregory was three. "His style is definitely masculine and he does some very intricate things that the average dancer can't even execute." LeTang, creator of show-stopping numbers for Hines in the Broadway musicals *Eubie!* and *Sophisticated Ladies,* and in the film *The Cotton Club,* says, "If I wanted him to leap off a chandelier, he'd do it. He can carry off whatever I dream up."

Hines is also blessed with an easy charm and genuineness that make him extremely attractive onstage and on-screen. After five movies, though, he still doesn't claim to have mastered the craft of film acting. "I'm feeling better about it," he says, "and I'm happy to say I'm getting more practice at it, but the most relaxed I feel is when I'm dancing."

Born in Harlem and raised in Brooklyn, the dancing Hines Kids made their nightclub debut at ages five and seven; their Broadway debut came three years later in the musical *The Girl in Pink Tights.* They continued touring as the Hines Brothers and later Hines, Hines, and Dad for more than twenty years, before splitting up in 1973. A burned-out Gregory spent the next five years writing songs and doing odd jobs in Venice, California.

When he returned to New York, he quickly found work in a Broadway-bound musical called *The Last Minstrel Show.* It closed in Philadelphia, but *Eubie!,* a musical tribute to Eubie Blake, opened on Broadway several months later, earning Hines terrific reviews and a 1978 Tony nomination.

"IT'S NO SECRET THAT MR. HINES MAY BE THE BEST TAP DANCER OF OUR DAY, BUT HE'S NEVER HAD THE CHANCE TO SHOW HIMSELF TO QUITE THE ADVANTAGE HE DOES HERE. . . . HE'S MORE THAN A DANCER; HE'S THE FRISKY ELLINGTON SPIRIT INCARNATE. AND, LIKE THE SHOW'S UNSEEN HERO, HE SEEMS TO BE ABLE TO DO EVERYTHING—INCLUDING, AT ONE POINT, A SOLO ON THE DRUMS. THIS MAN IS HUMAN LIGHTNING, AND HE JUST CAN'T BE CONTAINED."

—FRANK RICH,
The New York Times

Sophisticated Ladies *(1981), Lunt-Fontanne Theater, New York*

Copyright © 1984 Bert Andrews

Eubie! *(1978), Ambassador Theatre, New York*

Copyright © 1984 Martha Swope

With Robert Jackson in Comin' Uptown *(1979), Winter Garden Theatre, New York*

"THE BEST THING ABOUT IT IS THE DANCING—TAP AND OTHERWISE—OF THE HINES BROTHERS, MAURICE AND GREGORY. GREGORY, MOREOVER, IS A SPLENDID COMIC ACTOR, AND WHATEVER HE DOES (EVEN THE SEMIPERMANENT WINK OF THE LEFT EYE WHILE THE RIGHT BEAMS AHEAD INGENUOUSLY) IS TOUCHED WITH THE COMELINESS OF TOTAL, EASEFUL ASSURANCE."

—JOHN SIMON,
New York

"GREGORY HINES . . . IS AN EXPLOSIVE FORCE AND SHOULD PROBABLY BE PATENTED. THE GUY'S TERRIFIC, WHETHER HE IS ACTING WITH WOEBEGONE GRACE, SINGING WITH A SOULLIKE BEAT AND A HEARTLIKE BLEAT, OR SIMPLY DANCING UP HURRICANE GREGORY AND SUGGESTING HE IS THE BEST TAP DANCER IN THE WORLD SINCE BILL ROBINSON."

—CLIVE BARNES,
New York Post

His next musical, *Comin' Uptown* (1979), retold Dickens's *A Christmas Carol* with an all-black cast and a contemporary Harlem setting. The show flopped, but Hines received another set of terrific reviews and another Tony nomination for his performance as Scrooge, the neighborhood slumlord.

Copyright © 1981 Brooksfilms Ltd.; released by Twentieth Century-Fox

With Mel Brooks in
History of the World, Part I *(1981)*

Copyright © 1981 Orion Pictures Corporation

Wolfen *(1981)*

"IT'S INSPIRED TO CAST A DANCER LIKE HINES AS A MEDICAL SPECIALIST, BECAUSE HE BRINGS STARTLING ENERGY TO WHAT COULD HAVE BEEN A SEDENTARY PERFORMANCE. HINES ALL BUT CUTS CAPERS AROUND HIS MICROSCOPE: HE DANCES, HIS SILVER EARRING DANCES, THE SCREEN DANCES."

—CARRIE RICKEY,
The Village Voice

"THE MARVELOUS BLACK DANCER GREGORY HINES SHOWS UP CLAIMING TO BE JEWISH AND DOES A SUAVELY RELAXED SOFT SHOE."

—DAVID DENBY,
New York

In the following year, Hines made his first movie, playing a medical examiner opposite Albert Finney in the suspense thriller *Wolfen*. "I didn't have much of an idea of what I was doing," he says now, but it doesn't show in his performance. He continued stealing scenes as a dancing Roman slave in his second movie, Mel Brooks's *History of the World, Part I.*

Both films were released in the summer of 1981, soon after Hines opened in a musical that was, at last, worthy of his talent—*Sophisticated Ladies.* The show, a lavish salute to Duke Ellington, had been termed a disaster in its Washington, D.C., tryout. Hines was fired and then quickly rehired; the director soon left the show.

After a miraculous overhaul by San Francisco Ballet artistic director Michael Smuin, *Sophisticated Ladies* arrived on Broadway in triumph. The excitement Hines generated tapping up and down a lighted staircase and singing half a dozen Ellington songs in a satiny voice reached all the way to the top of the Lunt-Fontanne's second balcony.

"Gregory and I collaborated a great deal on the show," says Smuin. "We were a good team. He doesn't like to rehearse too much, but he loves to perform and wants to get things absolutely right. He's a wonderful, natural dancer—the black Fred Astaire."

Smuin, LeTang, and Hines reteamed for *The Cotton Club,* the forty-eight-million-dollar film extravaganza that made *Sophisticated Ladies* seem like a picnic in Central Park. "It was madness," says Smuin, "but so much fun to work on. Sometimes I would do a number in the morning and we'd shoot it that afternoon."

"I was starting to think it was *me,*" jokes Hines of the turmoil surrounding both projects. "But all those memories are really positive memories. Ultimately we got something we could be proud of."

Perhaps the best thing about *The Cotton Club* was the showcase it provided for Gregory Hines's tapping. "Dancing live, I sometimes have to censor what I do," he points out. "I'm not physically able to do certain steps eight times a week. In a movie, I can do it all day and then collapse.

"Of course," he adds, "there's no substitute for dancing in front of people and feeling and hearing that response from them. As much as I enjoy doing movies, that's a strong pull to get back to. And I really like the life of performing on Broadway—it's like having a steady job. You get a night off, and they actually give you a paid vacation!"

Hines was away from the theater for more than three years making *The Cotton Club, The Deal of the Century* (a 1983 comedy flop about arms trading), and *White Nights,* a 1985 release co-starring Mikhail Baryshnikov. In *White Nights,* Hines plays a Vietnam-veteran dancer who defects to the Soviet Union; Baryshnikov is a Russian dancer who returns home. Of their partnership, Hines quips, "I taught him how to do a little bit of tapping, and he taught me how to drink vodka."

With his wife, producer Pamela Koslow, Hines is developing a musical about the life and times of Jelly Roll Morton. "I want to do things with real substance and depth," he says. "I don't want to dance for joy all the time, I want to tap-dance pain and anger and

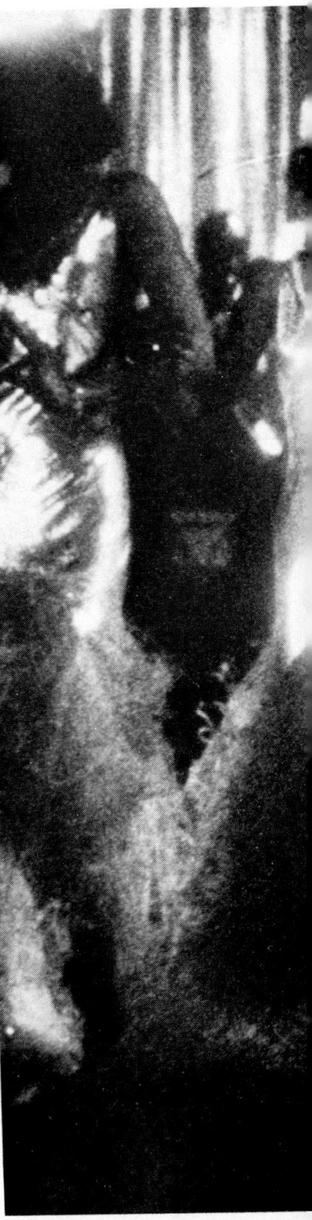

Adger W. Cowans

love and romance and even sensuality. It's important to me to bring more to the musical than just music."

Having spent his entire life in show business, Hines says he feels optimistic about the status of black performers these days. "There's a lot of inequity, but I'd rather get past that and focus on the positive," he says. "The roles are there, it's just a question of pressure and desire to get those roles."

Talent and desire have certainly carried Gregory Hines a long way. "I really love to dance," he says simply. "I think I'm going to dance till I can't."

"THE SCREEN VIBRATES WITH JUICY CHARACTERIZATIONS. . . . HINES IS A STUPENDOUS DANCER AND A DELIGHTFUL, BIGHEARTED ACTOR."

—JACK KROLL, *Newsweek*

The Cotton Club *(1984)*

Mary Beth Hurt

Onstage, Mary Beth Hurt has displayed an amazing range in works by Molière, Congreve, Shakespeare, Chekhov, Soviet playwright Victor Rozov, and Beth Henley, among others. "I've seen her play the most eccentric roles," says Joseph Papp, who gave Hurt her start as a ninety-eight-year-old Vietnamese man in the black comedy *More Than You Deserve.* "People think of her as serious, but she's a wonderful comedienne—she can go to either extreme."

As Papp notes, moviegoers have seen only the more somber, buttoned-in side of Mary Beth Hurt. Ironically, her film characters—in *Interiors, Head Over Heels,* and *The World According to Garp*—were also the ones that Hurt found most challenging to play.

"The closer a role is to me, the harder it is," she says. "There's less of a mask, less of a structure to build." Unlike many actors, she doesn't seem to mind the anonymity of the mask: "I'm rarely recognized, and that's great fun." Nor does she mind being known as a character actor: "That's what I am, what I've always been, and what I always want to be."

A native of Marshalltown, Iowa, Hurt [the name from her early marriage to actor William Hurt] had little trouble establishing herself in the theater after graduating from the NYU School of the Arts. "I didn't audition for anything for six months because I was afraid of being rejected," she recalls. Once she did, she was quickly cast in *More Than You Deserve,* and one plum role followed another.

She played Celia in the Public Theater's Central Park version of *As You Like It,* then spent two seasons with New York's Phoenix Theater Company alongside actors such as Meryl Streep, Glenn Close, and John Lithgow. "I don't think anybody knew we would have the careers that we've had," she says. Yet she won the

"AS MEG, THE LOOSE, SELFISH SISTER WHO BLOSSOMED TOO EARLY, MISS HURT PROVES SHE'S A POWERFULLY SEXY COMEDIENNE AS WELL AS A GOOD ACTRESS. A BATTLE-SCARRED, RUEFUL ADULT, SHE ALSO LETS US SEE THE GOLDEN, HEADSTRONG TEENAGE GIRL WHO ONCE LIKED TO SHOCK HER PEERS BY MOCKING THE MARCH OF DIMES POSTERS AT DIXIE-LAND DRUGS."

—Frank Rich,
The New York Times

Crimes of the Heart *(1981), Golden Theater, New York*

Clarence Derwent Award as New York's most promising female actor for her role in Congreve's *Love for Love* and a Tony nomination for the Public's production of *Trelawny of the Wells,* co-starring Streep, Lithgow, and Mandy Patinkin. Her repertory work in the melodrama *Secret Service* and the farce *Boy Meets Girl* led *New York Times* critic Walter Kerr to begin one of his 1976 Sunday columns by asking: "Why not just call this Mary Beth Hurt Week and let it go at that?"

Behind Hurt's varied performances lies "a keen analytical mind," says Joseph Papp, "plus—pardon me saying so—a kind of hurt. There's something in her psyche that can experience pain, and she manages to convey that to an audience so that you identify with her."

That quality is quite evident in her work as the youngest sister in Woody Allen's *Interiors* (1978) and the object of obsessive love in Joan Micklin Silver's *Head Over Heels* (1979), rereleased three years later with a different ending as *Chilly Scenes of Winter*.

"MAYBE BEST OF ALL IS MARY BETH HURT AS UNCLE REMUS (BLOODY MARY), WHO OBSEQUIOUSLY, SARDONICALLY, AND HILARIOUSLY SURVIVES COUNTLESS BULLET AND KNIFE WOUNDS WITH THE FORTITUDE OF MOTHER COURAGE."

—Douglas Watt, New York *Daily News*

George E. Joseph

With Leata Galloway in More Than You Deserve *(1974), Public Theater, New York*

"THE EVENING IS STOLEN BY A SLIP OF A THING NAMED MARY BETH HURT, AN INNOCENT HIKING HER SKIRTS UP AS THOUGH SHE'S JUST COME FROM THE BUTTER CHURN, PEERING THROUGH SPECTACLES TO APPROVE ANY FOP WHO WILL HAVE HER."

—WALTER KERR, *The New York Times*

Copyright Van Williams

Love for Love *(1974), Helen Hayes Theater, New York*

"Mary Beth is a real person," says Silver, "and I thought that would make the story more interesting than using a cover-girl type. She works very carefully and really thinks about the emotional life of the character. I like the concentration that stage actors bring to film work."

Moviemaking provides a real test of that concentration, according to Hurt. "I think film is more difficult [than theater]," she says, "because you don't have the luxury of going from beginning to end. You have to pick up in the middle, or at the end, and some days you just can't seem to do it. When that happens on the stage, you can say, 'Too bad, I can't do it tonight, but I'm going to have innumerable other chances.' That's not true of film."

George E. Joseph

Trelawny of the Wells *(1975),*
Vivian Beaumont Theater, New York

"MISS HURT IS VERY APPEALING AS THE YOUNGEST DAUGHTER WHO HATES HER MOTHER AND, THUS, GOES OUT OF HER WAY TO CONVINCE HERSELF SHE DOESN'T."

—VINCENT CANBY,
The New York Times

Copyright © 1978 United Artists Corporation

With Sam Waterston in Interiors *(1978)*

"THE ACTING WAS DOMINATED BY MISS HURT AS ROSE TRELAWNY—SWEET, TOUCHING, PETULANT, AND FUNNY, HER FACE, HER VOICE, HER GESTURES WERE JUST RIGHT."

—CLIVE BARNES,
The New York Times

In her next movie, Hurt, who'd just passed thirty, played the teenage daughter of Shirley MacLaine and Anthony Hopkins in *A Change of Seasons.* (She was believable; the movie was not and was swiftly forgotten.) Returning to the stage, she took on a very different role—the flashy, tart-tongued Meg MaGrath in Beth Henley's *Crimes of the Heart.* The play premiered at the Manhattan Theatre Club, then moved to Broadway after Henley won the 1981 Pulitzer Prize.

Though Hurt received a Tony nomination for her performance, she says, "I don't think I would have been given the chance to play Meg if the show had originated on Broadway." Indeed, she'd originally been called in to play Babe, the self-absorbed sister who shoots her husband. "There's much more freedom to experiment Off-Broadway," she notes. "If there isn't as much money involved, the producer and director are willing to let you try things."

"THERE IS ONE EXQUISITE PERFORMANCE IN *BOY MEETS GIRL.* MARY BETH HURT AS SUSIE, HAPPY'S MOTHER, IS NOT JUST A DUMB BLONDE; SHE IS A DAINTY, INNOCENT ROSEBUD, SWEET, GIRLISH, SENSITIVE, AND SINCERE. A LOVABLE GOODNESS RADIATES FROM HER."

—JULIUS NOVICK,
The Village Voice

Copyright Van Williams

With Don Scardino in Boy Meets Girl *(1976), Playhouse Theatre, New York*

"HEARD IS WELL MATCHED WITH HURT, WHO IS GENTLY MOVING AS A MODEST, MILD-MANNERED WOMAN TORN BETWEEN LOYALTY TO HER HUSBAND AND HER NEED FOR LOVE."

—KATHLEEN CARROLL, New York *Daily News*

Copyright © 1979 United Artists Corporation

With John Heard in Head Over Heels *(1979)*

"GARP'S WIFE IS THE MOST REALISTICALLY CONCEIVED CHARACTER, AND SHE COULD EASILY HAVE BEEN WIPED OFF THE SCREEN BY ALL THE COLORFUL GROTESQUES, BUT MARY BETH HURT ENDOWS HER WITH A HUMANITY THAT IS DEEPLY APPEALING."

—DAVID ANSEN, *Newsweek*

Impressed with her performance in *Crimes,* George Roy Hill cast Hurt as Helen Holm, true love of T. S. Garp in *The World According to Garp.* Hers was one of the least showy roles in the film, but she played it with strength and subtlety. "A beautiful job," Hill says simply.

Copyright Christian Simonpietri/Sygma

With Robin Williams in The World According to Garp *(1982)*

A three-month run in Molière's *The Misanthrope* followed, where Hurt was faced with the challenge of speaking in rhymed couplets. "I didn't get my feet into that role until halfway through the run," she says, "but once I did, I had fun and felt quite at home. It was like being a figure skater."

A year later, after having a baby daughter with her film-director husband Paul Schrader, Hurt won warm reviews as a disillusioned daughter in Victor Rozov's *The Nest of the Wood Grouse* under Joseph Papp's direction. "Theater feeds me in a way that continues to feel good," she says, explaining her loyalty to the stage. "It's been very loyal to me."

Hurt got back into films as well in the fall of 1984 with a small part in Frank Perry's *Compromising Positions.* "I've been extremely lucky," she says. "There are always things that could have gone a little better, but as far as my life and my career are concerned, it could be going much, much worse."

With Brian Bedford in The Misanthrope *(1983), Circle in the Square Theatre, New York*

"MARY BETH HURT IS SUCH AN ADORABLY SEXY CELIMENE THAT ONE NEVER WONDERS WHY THE WORLD ADORES HER."

—CLIVE BARNES, *New York Post*

Copyright © 1984 Martha Swope

William Hurt

William Hurt's work in *Altered States* and *Body Heat* made him a movie star, but Hurt was more interested in fresh acting challenges than in fame. In a ten-year career, he has played Hamlet and a lovesick janitor, Lord Byron and a coke-snorting casting director, a Russian police investigator and a jailed Argentinian homosexual. "For me," says Hurt, "to choose to repeat is not a choice."

"Bill Hurt is the most unpredictable actor I know," producer Joseph Papp says admiringly. "He makes choices you would never think about, which requires a very unusual imagination. I've never seen a better performance of his than in *The Big Chill,* and yet contrast that with what he did in the park as Oberon in *A Midsummer Night's Dream*—I can't think of anybody around like him."

Born in Washington, D.C., Hurt spent his early childhood in the South Pacific, where his father worked for the State Department. When his parents divorced and his mother married Henry Luce III, he was sent to Middlesex prep school in Massachusetts. He entered Tufts University in 1968 as a theology major, switched to drama after his junior year, and spent his senior year studying acting in London. Admitted to Juilliard in 1972, he dropped out before his fourth year in confusion over his professional goals and his personal life, and took off cross-country on a motorcycle.

Hurt ended up at the Oregon Shakespearean Festival, where he acted in three plays, including *Long Day's Journey into Night* in which he played Edmund. "That was the first time I acted, in my own estimation," he says. When he returned to New York, he played Lord Scroop and two other minor roles in Joseph Papp's 1976 Central Park production of *Henry V.* "He mumbled then," Papp recalls. "I said, 'Can't you speak up?' "

The following winter, Hurt began his most important theatrical relationship, with director Marshall Mason and the Off-Broadway

"HAMLET ALLOWS WILLIAM HURT, ONE OF OUR MOST GIFTED YOUNG ACTORS, TO EXPAND HIS RANGE AND TO INVESTIGATE HIS EMOTIONAL RESOURCES. AMONG OTHER THINGS, MR. HURT IS A VERY AMUSING AND PRANKISH HAMLET, THE WITTY SUPERIOR TO ALL THE LESS KNOWING KNIGHTS IN THE REALM. MR. HURT DELIVERS SOME OF THE SOLILOQUIES WITH QUIET CONVICTION, AS DEEPLY PERSONAL CONFIDENCES. IN THE BEST SENSE, THE ACTOR IS UNPREDICTABLE."

—Mel Gussow,
The New York Times

Hamlet *(1979), Circle Repertory Company, New York*

Circle Repertory Company. He was cast as the lead in Corinne Jacker's *My Life,* a play about a scientist who tries to examine the roots of human behavior.

"I felt like I had finally come home," Hurt says of Circle Rep. "For most of my life, I had felt estranged. The idea of Circle Rep, the way they were working, was exactly what I had been hoping for for so long."

Hank Kranzler

Long Day's Journey into Night *(1975), Oregon Shakespearean Festival, Ashland, Oregon*

"EDMUND TYRONE, THE SON WHO IS REALLY O'NEILL HIMSELF, IS TROUBLED MORE WITH PHYSICAL THAN PSYCHOLOGICAL AILMENTS. . . . IT'S A ROLE THAT CALLS FOR UNDERPLAYING, FOR QUIET UNDERSTANDING, AND THIS IS WHAT WILLIAM HURT GIVES TO THE PART."

—DON BISHOFF,
Eugene Register-Guard, Eugene, Oregon

"WILLIAM HURT PLAYS EDWARD, IN ALL HIS FRUSTRATION, WITH QUIET STRENGTH AND EMOTION AND WITH SOME HUMOR, TOO."

—EDITH OLIVER,
The New Yorker

Copyright © 1984 Ken Howard

My Life *(1977), Circle Repertory Company, New York*

Copyright © 1984 Gerry Goodstein

Childe Byron *(1981), Circle Repertory Company, New York*

"ALL THE ACTORS GLIDED THROUGH THE PLAY WITH UNDERSTATED ELEGANCE—IF I PICK OUT WILLIAM HURT AS THE CRIPPLED VIETNAM VETERAN, HE IS SIMPLY AN EXAMPLE FROM AN ENSEMBLE WHERE EVERYONE MURMURS AND MUTTERS POETRY IN TUNE WITH THE PLAYWRIGHT'S SONG."

—CLIVE BARNES,
New York Post

Copyright © 1984 Ken Howard

With Jeff Daniels in Fifth of July *(1978), Circle Repertory Company, New York*

"MR. HURT CHARGES THROUGH THIS PLAY WITH HIS HEAD THROWN BACK AND HIS FACE IN AN ALMOST FACETIOUS GRIN, AS IF LIFE WERE A GRAND JOKE CREATED FOR HIS PERSONAL AMUSEMENT. WHAT MAKES THIS TALENTED ACTOR SO SPECIAL—AND, INEVITABLY, A STAR—IS HIS ABILITY TO CREATE HIS OWN REALITY ONSTAGE. THE HERO HE CREATES IN *CHILDE BYRON* IS AS AMERICAN AND CONTEMPORARY AS STANLEY KOWALSKI—AND MUCH FUNNIER."

—FRANK RICH,
The New York Times

Recalls Marshall Mason, "It was like falling in love. By the end of the first rehearsal, we knew that we were meant to work together forever. He is a great actor."

Hurt won an Obie Award for *My Life* and performed in four other plays during 1977–78 at Circle Rep, most notably the original production of Lanford Wilson's *Fifth of July.* That body of work, along with PBS appearances in *The Best of Families* and *Verna: USO Girl,* brought the movie scripts.

"I had turned down film for a long time, knowing that things would change in my life," Hurt says. "I value privacy, and I like to be able to do things without being judged. But I had to do *Altered*

Copyright © 1980 Warner Bros. Inc.

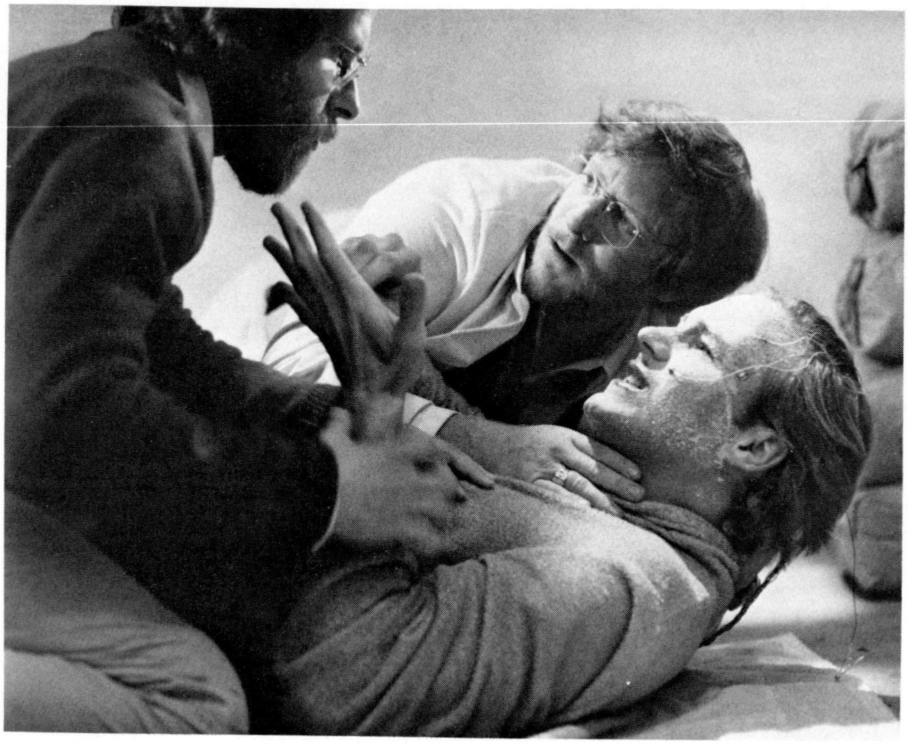

With Bob Balaban and Charles Haid in Altered States *(1980)*

"APPEARING IN MOVIES FOR THE FIRST TIME, THE ARTFUL YOUNG STAGE ACTOR WILLIAM HURT BRINGS NUANCES TO HIS REVVED-UP MAD-SCIENTIST ROLE BY ACTING SLIGHTLY WITHDRAWN AND INHUMAN. . . . HURT HOLDS BACK JUST ENOUGH; HE MAKES EDDIE THE KIND OF CUNNING MANIAC WHO'S ALWAYS WATCHING TO SEE HOW PEOPLE REACT TO HIS MANIA. HE'S NEURASTHENIC, CHARISMATIC, AND READY TO TRY ANYTHING."

—PAULINE KAEL,
The New Yorker

States—Paddy Chayefsky was my hero and it was a brilliant piece. So I was off to the races."

Within a year, three films starring William Hurt had been released: *Altered States,* the story of a scientist's obsessive search for his true self; *Eyewitness,* a stylish romantic thriller in which Hurt, a janitor, falls in love with newscaster Sigourney Weaver; and *Body Heat,* Lawrence Kasdan's *film noir* drama pairing Hurt with newcomer Kathleen Turner.

In each movie, Hurt brought what critic Vincent Canby calls "a character actor's particularity" to his leading-man roles. The actor himself says he doesn't think of roles in terms of their size. "A good production is one where if you look at the spear carrier for a minute, you have a window into the whole play," he says. "I had as much fun working on three small roles in *Henry V* in the park for Joe Papp as I did in a lot of supposedly more enviable situations."

With fame pressing in, Hurt found refuge at Circle Rep, winning warm reviews for his Hamlet. "That production was something to be proud of," he says, "because we *did* the play [straight, without gimmicks]. I truly do feel good when the play is being served. In the theater, you don't try to manipulate feelings—you simply drop yourself, listen to the play, and hope that that

Copyright © 1982 Jean Pagliuso/Visages

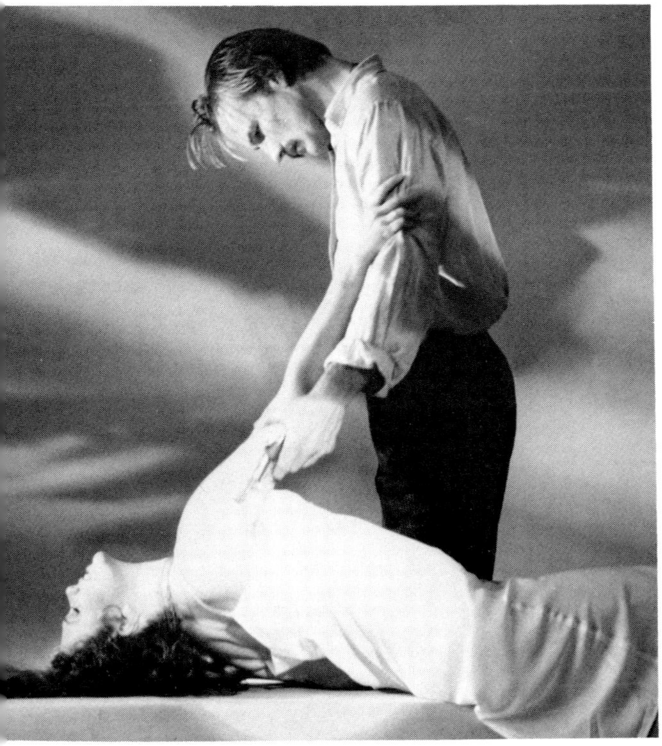

With Kathleen Turner in *Body Heat (1982)*

"FOR AN ACTOR TRAINED IN STAGE WORK, HURT HAS REMARKABLE ECONOMY OF GESTURE. HE ACTS WITH HIS EYES AND HIS VOICE: UNDER PRESSURE, HIS HEAD SNAPS INTO A STARE THAT MEANS TO BURN INTO THE VIEWER'S SKULL, AND HIS VOICE EXHALES INTELLECTUAL URGENCY, AS IF A DANGEROUS POSSIBILITY HAD JUST SLAPPED HIM ON THE BACK."

—RICHARD CORLISS,
Time

Copyright © 1983 Columbia Pictures Industries, Inc.

With Mary Kay Place in *The Big Chill (1983)*

"ONLY THE POWER OF HURT'S COLD-FEVER PERFORMANCE MAKES US OVERLOOK THE HEAVY-HANDEDNESS OF HIS SYMBOLIC EMASCULATION."

—DAVID ANSEN,
Newsweek

contributes [to the audience's understanding]."

On the night before *Eyewitness* was released, Hurt opened at Circle Rep in *Childe Byron,* giving a magnetic performance in a rather weak play. A year later, he and Circle Rep were less successful with a production of *Richard II* set in pre-Christian Celtic England. (It never opened.) Hurt nevertheless cites it as one of his biggest challenges.

Joseph Papp then asked him to return to Central Park in the 1982 production of *A Midsummer Night's Dream.* The critics were divided on his performance as Oberon, some of them questioning his pauses and emphasis on certain dialogue, but he made a striking impression. Hurt calls the play "an irresistible force—the humor and compassion of it just keep bubbling up. But unless the wind blew, I found it difficult to conjure the play, which Oberon must do."

Papp considered Hurt's work "extraordinary—I'd hear his reading of the lines and say, 'My God, that's wrong,' but it wasn't, because he made it work for him."

Two years passed between the release of *Body Heat* and *The Big Chill,* in which Lawrence Kasdan wrote the part of a cynical Vietnam veteran especially for Hurt. Kasdan calls him "one of the great actors of my generation," and Hurt returns the admiration, noting with some bitterness that *The Big Chill* was turned down by several studios before being made by Columbia. "The ideas underlying *Big Chill* are definitive," he says. "It was a wonderfully constructed piece of work."

Hurt deflects praise of his performance in *The Big Chill,* but he was, in fact, wonderfully funny in a difficult part, especially the scene in which his character, a psychologist, analyzes himself on videotape. Several months later, he drew mixed reviews as a Russian investigator in *Gorky Park,* a film that lacked the verve of the best-selling novel on which it was based.

For Hurt, 1984 became the year of *Hurlyburly.* As Eddie, a confused, misogynistic Hollywood casting director, he was the fulcrum for David Rabe's three-hour-long play. Other characters came and went, but Eddie was onstage in every scene, and Hurt interacted beautifully with all of his co-stars. He stayed with the

"WILLIAM HURT'S HUMOROUS, SERIOUS OBERON IS QUIETLY ELEGANT—HIS SILENT PRESENCE (AS HE WATCHES THE YOUNG LOVERS' SCRAPPING AND SHAKESPEARE'S VARIOUS OTHER SHENANIGANS) BEING AS DYNAMIC AS HIS BEAUTIFULLY SPOKEN WORDS."

—EDITH OLIVER, *The New Yorker*

Copyright © 1984 Susan Cook/Martha Swope Associates

With Marcell Rosenblatt in A Midsummer Night's Dream *(1982), Delacorte Theater, Central Park*

"WILLIAM HURT IS VERY LIKABLY AUTHORITATIVE AS THE RUSSIAN INVESTIGATOR."

—ANDREW SARRIS,
The Village Voice

Copyright © 1983 Eagle Associates

Gorky Park *(1983)*

exhausting role through three months in Chicago, three months Off-Broadway, and four months on Broadway. "It took that long to feel I had done what I could," he says. "It's a great play, greater perhaps than we yet know."

Before entering *Hurlyburly,* Hurt had filmed a starring role in Brazilian director Hector Babenco's *Kiss of the Spider Woman,* based on a Manuel Puig novel. He plays a homosexual window dresser who entertains cellmate Raul Julia with tales from the movies. Babenco told *American Film* magazine that he had seen Hurt turn down three movie deals that would have each paid him a million dollars. "Being an actor means for him, in my comprehension, a step in his own life," Babenco said.

Hurt's devotion to his craft, his "love of the work for its own sake," comes through in everything he says. "Jason Robards has said, 'Acting is about telling the truth,'" he notes. "You can act in a film or you can act on the stage—the trappings are different, the goal is the same."

Copyright © 1984 Martha Swope

With Christopher Walken in Hurlyburly *(1984), Promenade Theatre, New York*

"IN THE TWO PERFORMANCES I SAW, WILLIAM HURT WAS TREMENDOUSLY IMPLOSIVE ONCE AND TREMENDOUSLY EXPLOSIVE ONCE. HE IS A CLEAR, POWERFUL CENTER FOR ONE OF THE BEST ENSEMBLE PERFORMANCES ON ANY AMERICAN STAGE."

—JACK KROLL,
Newsweek

Judith Ivey

For a good time in the theater, call Judith Ivey. Whether she's playing a Cockney working girl, a coke-snorting bubble dancer, or the wife of a vice-presidential candidate, Ivey delivers a performance from the heart—funny, touching, always human.

"Judy is brilliant at finding the humor in a character," says Carole Rothman, who directed her in the offbeat comic play *Pastorale* in 1982. "Through finding the humor, she finds the humanity, and that's what people respond to in her. She's got great comic timing, and she's never-ending in her inventiveness."

"I've been funny for as long as I can remember," says Ivey, who spent her early years in Odessa, Texas, then moved fifteen times because of her father's work as a college administrator. "That's the way I got along with people. I had glasses and was a beanpole, and since I couldn't be pretty per se, I made people laugh."

A high-school production of *The Man Who Came to Dinner* became Ivey's first big acting success. She majored in drama at Illinois State University, then settled in Chicago in 1973 and began building a comfortable career making commercials and acting at the Goodman Theatre. Five years later, she decided to move to New York.

"I was tired of playing the second lead and watching the leading lady come from New York," she recalls. "In some cases they'd even run to me and say, 'If we fire her, would you . . . ?' If nothing else, I thought I could get the leading-lady roles and then go back to Chicago."

Ivey found herself on Broadway within a year, in the British comedy *Bedroom Farce* (she'd developed an excellent ear for accents during her many childhood moves), having advanced from

"AS FOR JUDITH IVEY, SHE IS AN UNMITIGATED JOY. MISS IVEY MAKES JOSIE, A PLUM OF A PART, EVEN PLUMMIER, BRINGING OUT EFFORTLESSLY EVERY QUIRK, SHADING, AND MODULATION—EVERY STRENGTH AND WEAKNESS. THIS IS JOSIE IN ALL HER GAIETY, WISTFULNESS, AND TEEMING THREE-DIMENSIONALITY. TRULY, SERENDIPITOUS ACTING IN THE ROUND!"

—John Simon, *New York*

Steaming *(1982), Brooks Atkinson Theatre, New York*

"IT IS A BRAVURA ROLE, BUT IT IS ALSO FLAWED. THE BURDEN OF SHOWING CHANGE, THEREFORE, IS ON THE ACTRESS. HAPPILY, MISS IVEY UNDERSTANDS THIS. SHE GROWS IN THE PART."

—John Corry,
The New York Times

Copyright © 1984 Martha Swope

Piaf *(1981), Plymouth Theatre, New York*

understudy. Next, in *Piaf,* another British play, she began as understudy and ended up playing the lead during matinees. "I fought for that challenge because I knew it would be a big leap in my acting," she says. "I use it as a demarcation line of where I think my acting changed and I grew up."

A year later, however, Ivey seriously considered quitting. Though she'd received terrific reviews in *Pastorale* at the Off-Broadway Second Stage, and her work was respected in theatrical circles, she couldn't see a payoff.

"People were telling me I was the hottest young actress in New York City *while* I was standing in the unemployment line," she says. "I was the queen of workshops where they'd hand you three hundred forty bucks at the end of eight weeks. I was thirty years old and had watched my savings dwindle, and I began to wonder if this was going to be the extent of my career. I figured I'd become a pet-store owner and get my kicks that way."

Steaming put a stop to that idea. Ivey dazzled critics and audiences as Josie, a tarted-up Cockney who spends her spare time relaxing at a London Turkish bath. The part could have been a tough-chick stereotype, the nudity could have been self-conscious, but not with a sensitive actor like Ivey playing it. *Steaming*'s "feminist awakening" plot seemed almost old-fashioned by New York standards, and the play ran for only two months, but its star won a Tony, along with movie offers for amounts totaling considerably more than 340 bucks.

Copyright © 1982 Stephanie Saia

With Christine Estabrook in Pastorale *(1982), Second Stage, New York*

In a trio of 1984 releases, Ivey played Steve Martin's girlfriend in *The Lonely Guy,* a flirtatious secretary in Paul Newman's *Harry and Son,* and Gene Wilder's good-natured wife in *The Woman in Red.* None of the films fully captured her comedic gifts, but she found the process of movie acting satisfying.

"I like the smallness of it, making the character come across only so far," she says. "The hardest thing for me is not having an audience there as a barometer."

Ivey returned to the stage in yet another Off-Broadway workshop, a one-woman play she helped develop herself called

"MISS IVEY, ALWAYS A FIRST-RATE ACTRESS, GETS THE CHANCE TO WEAR RACY LINGERIE ON HER HEAD AND, IN GENERAL, TO SHOW OFF HER HIGH STYLE AS A COMEDIAN. CARVING UP A LEMON FOR HER GIN, SHE BRINGS DOWN THE HOUSE BY LAUGHINGLY ANNOUNCING, OF ALL THINGS, 'WHENEVER I DO THIS, I ALWAYS PICTURE THE BLADE IN MY HEART!' "

—Frank Rich,
The New York Times

Second Lady. It began with her character, the wife of a vice-presidential candidate, giving a standard campaign speech; it ended with the character's emotional collapse. Ivey calls *Second Lady* "another big leap in my acting. When your acting partner is the audience, you're never quite sure what will come your way each night. It really prepared me for the spontaneity required by *Hurlyburly.*"

The actress spent most of 1984 onstage playing a smart stripper in David Rabe's funny, unsparing look at life in Hollywood. While the *Hurlyburly* ensemble included William Hurt, Christopher Walken, and Sigourney Weaver, Ivey's troubled yet sensible character became the audience's favorite. "It's an amazing piece of writing," she says. "No matter how many times you do it, you hear something else and can explore that. You had to be wide open to

"JUDITH IVEY HAS A QUALITY OF TOTAL BELIEVABILITY NO MATTER HOW ALIEN THE CIRCUMSTANCES MAY BE TO HER IMMEDIATE EXPERIENCE. SHE AVOIDS ARTIFICE AND MANNERISMS AT THE SAME TIME THAT SHE PERSONIFIES CHARACTERS. THIS IS VERY MUCH THE CASE IN *SECOND LADY*, FINELY TAILORED TO MISS IVEY'S EXCEPTIONAL TALENT. WE FEEL THE INSECURITY, CANDOR, AND EMOTIONAL TURMOIL BEHIND THE POLITESSE."

—MEL GUSSOW,
The New York Times

George Connolly

Second Lady *(1983), Production Company, New York*

Courtesy of Universal Pictures

With Steve Martin in The Lonely Guy *(1984)*

Hurlyburly *(1984), Promenade Theatre, New York*

Copyright © 1984 Martha Swope

"JUDITH IVEY IS LOVELY AS A SIX-TIME DIVORCEÉ IN LOVE WITH LARRY."

—Hank Gallo,
New York *Daily News*

"JUDITH IVEY IS SO PHENOMENAL THAT SHE CAN PLAY TABLE TENNIS WITH YOUR HEART AND BE AT BOTH ENDS OF THE TABLE SIMULTANEOUSLY."

—John Simon,
New York

whatever might happen—it was real moment-to-moment acting."

As director Carole Rothman notes, "Whatever the character is, Judy will go out and be it. She's gone onstage without her clothes on, and she's gone onstage a little overweight because she thought the character of the stripper should look that way. She's very brave."

She's also not content to sit back and bask in her success. In the fall of 1984, while acting in *Hurlyburly* eight times a week, Ivey performed the lead in a workshop of a new musical called *Philco Blues* and acted in Frank Perry's film of the Susan Isaacs best seller *Compromising Positions.* All three projects were simply too exciting to pass up.

She sang nine songs in *Philco,* the story of a Nebraska woman who becomes obsessed with a soap-opera star. (Ivey hopes to star in a full-scale production of the show in 1985.) In *Compromising Positions,* she plays a rich Texas-born sculptor, the best friend of the lead character, portrayed by Susan Sarandon.

"It's my favorite part in the four films I've done," she says. "This time, I finally trusted that I was being funny and that the director would put it together in a way that would embrace all I invested in the work."

Frank Perry calls Ivey "a genius—she's a consummate technician, an actor I'd been watching with pleasure on the stage." Perry deeply admires Ivey's commitment to a career that includes both stage and screen work. "In the past, a performer like Judy would have gone straight to Hollywood after *The Woman in Red,*" he says. "This generation of actors really is different."

With Gene Wilder in The Woman in Red *(1984)*

Copyright © 1984 Orion Pictures Corporation

"MISS IVEY AND [GILDA] RADNER BOTH PLAY STRAIGHT WOMEN TO MR. WILDER'S AMIABLE TEDDY, AND BOTH OF THEM PLAY IT SOMEWHAT DUMB. (MISS IVEY DOES A FINE JOB AND HAS AN EASIER TIME OF IT THAN DOES MISS RADNER. . . .)"

—JANET MASLIN, *The New York Times*

Says Ivey, "In the same way that I would never turn down a movie I wanted to do, I would never leave the stage. I couldn't live if I couldn't do theater. That immediate exchange with an audience, regardless of whether it's a comedy or a drama, is just everything to me."

Copyright © 1984 Ken Howard

Compromising Positions *(1985)*

Kevin Kline

Equally at home with Shakespeare, musicals, knockabout comedy, and romantic leading roles, Kevin Kline has become "a modern classical actor," in Joseph Papp's words. The fact that he is thirty-eight years old and spent eight years training and then touring with Juilliard's Acting Company before entering the world of commercial theater and movies merely underscores his seriousness about the craft of acting.

"Everything Kevin does, he thinks about and ponders and agonizes over for months," says Wilford Leach, his director in two acclaimed Public Theater productions, *The Pirates of Penzance* (1980) and *Henry V* (1984). "He wouldn't be as well trained as he is and, in a sense, as old as he is and just now becoming widely recognized if he hadn't stuck true to his vision of what he wanted to do. He has built a career that is going to last him a good long lifetime."

Kline grew up in St. Louis, the son of a record- and toy-store owner who encouraged his interest in the piano. After attending a boys' high school run by Benedictine monks, he entered Indiana University as a music major, hoping to become a composer and conductor. A freshman acting class led to a role in *Macbeth,* followed by a summer performing on a riverboat, followed by a switch to the drama department.

In 1968, Kline became one of the original students at the Juilliard Theater Center, established under John Houseman's artistic direction. Four years later, he and thirteen others graduated and stayed together to form the Acting Company, a touring repertory group. Traveling by bus, they performed both classic and modern plays in cities and towns all over the country. During his four years with the company, Kline played lead roles in *Ring 'Round the Moon, The School for Scandal, She Stoops to Conquer,*

"FROM THE MOMENT OF HIS FIRST ENTRANCE, HE IS ENTIRELY IN COMMAND: THE STRONGEST AND MOST INTELLIGENT PERSON IN THE PLAY. (MOST HENRIES V CAN MANAGE THE STRENGTH; NOT ALL CAN DO SO WELL AS MR. KLINE WITH THE INTELLIGENCE.) . . . MR. KLINE'S RIGOROUSLY UNDERSTATED PERFORMANCE IS NEVER DULL. AS THE CHARACTER HOLDS HIS ARMY, HIS COURT, HIS KINGDOM, BY INBORN STRENGTH AND MAGNETISM, SO DOES THE ACTOR HOLD HIS AUDIENCE."

—JULIUS NOVICK,
The Village Voice

Henry V *(1984), Delacorte Theater, Central Park*

The Three Sisters, and *The Robber Bridegroom,* among others.

"He really believed—we all believed—that this was the way to become a major actor," says Margot Harley, executive producer of the Acting Company. "He certainly could have gone out and worked; he was sought after during those last two years, but he stayed because he believed in the process."

Having watched the development of dozens of young actors, Harley acknowledges that she saw something special in Kevin Kline. "He's not only an extraordinary actor, he's also enormously charming, he has great charisma, and he's terribly handsome. Put those things together and you obviously think there's potential for a star."

After leaving the group, Kline worked on the soap opera *Search for Tomorrow* for a year, understudied Raul Julia in *The*

Copyright Diane Gorodnitzki

With Mary-Joan Negro in Ring 'Round the Moon *(1972), The Acting Company, Juilliard Theater Center*

Copyright Diane Gorodnitzki

She Stoops to Conquer *(1975), The Acting Company, Juilliard Theater Center*

Threepenny Opera at Lincoln Center, and had a small role in the 1977 Broadway production of *The Robber Bridegroom.* Then he took another small part and turned it into a Tony Award–winning show-stopper: Bruce Granit, a bumbling matinee idol who seduces Madeline Kahn in *On the Twentieth Century* (1978).

"Kevin auditioned via the casting department, and I thought he was sensational," recalls director Harold Prince. "It was the hardest part in the world to cast because I wanted somebody who was sophisticated and yet a farceur, which is a style we don't do plays in anymore. All I had to do was touch on that and he ran with the ball. We had about as much fun as I've ever had working with an actor."

As contradictory as it sounds, Kline indeed managed to execute a variety of pratfalls as well as to sing and romance the star with both elegance and panache. His next role, the lead in Michael Weller's *Loose Ends* at Circle in the Square, was a complete turnaround. He played a disillusioned former Peace Corps volunteer who questions the conventions of marriage and career-building in the seventies. The performance was understated and moving, and it helped establish Kline's versatility.

"Immediately after *Twentieth Century,* he was asked to star in a revival of a forties musical," says Harold Prince, "but he wisely did not allow himself to be pigeonholed. He doesn't deserve it and it didn't happen. It was perfectly fine two shows later to swashbuckle for laughs, but that straight play was very important for him."

No one could have predicted the triumphant success of *The Pirates of Penzance,* in which Kevin Kline swashbuckled for laughs in Central Park and later on Broadway, winning his second Tony. Critical response was ecstatic, and Kline soon found himself recipient of one of the most coveted movie roles in years, the tormented Nathan in *Sophie's Choice.*

"[KLINE'S] LINES ARE READ INCISIVELY, WITH SUCH INTELLECTUAL INTENSITY AND WIT THAT CLICHÉ IS DRIVEN FROM THEM. . . . THE ACTOR'S TIMING IS SO IMPECCABLE THAT HE CAN ARRIVE AT ONE FIRMLY OUTLINED CONCLUSION AND THEN, AFTER A SINGLE SUSPENSEFUL BEAT, DRAW A DEEPLY SATISFYING LAUGH BY ADDING AN EQUALLY FIRM 'PRIMARILY.' YOU KNOW THAT THE SELF-QUESTIONING IS BEGINNING ALL OVER AGAIN."

—WALTER KERR,
The New York Times

Copyright © 1984 Martha Swope

With Madeline Kahn in On the Twentieth Century *(1978), St. James Theatre, New York*

"A NEWCOMER NAMED KEVIN KLINE ALL BUT STEALS THE ENTIRE EVENING AS THE LOTHARIO TRAVELLING WITH MS. KAHN. HIS TIMING IS IMPECCABLE, HIS PROFILE IS ALWAYS TILTED FOR THAT POSSIBLE CLOSEUP, AND MUCH IS MADE OF A SERIES OF DOORS SMASHING IN HIS FACE THAT IS WORTH THE PRICE OF ADMISSION ALONE."

—REX REED,
New York *Daily News*

Copyright Bernard Gotfryd

With Roxanne Hart in Loose Ends *(1979), Circle in the Square Theatre, New York*

"KEVIN KLINE IS A SPECTACULAR PIRATE KING, WITH THE POSITIVELY CULINARY KNACK OF GLAZING EVERY BIT OF HAM WITH THE PUREST GOLDEN HONEY. UNLEASHED, HE CAN MAKE AN EPILEPTIC FIT LOOK LIKE THE MEREST PETIT MAL AND CONVULSE THE AUDIENCE ALONG WITH HIMSELF; RESTRAINED, HIS SILENT GAZE STILL CHURNS ABOUT IN HIS HEAD LIKE A TETHERED ROGUE ELEPHANT. WHATEVER HE DOES IS DONE WITH EQUAL AMOUNT OF DELIRIOUSNESS AND DECORUM."

—JOHN SIMON,
New York

Copyright © 1984 Martha Swope

The Pirates of Penzance *(1980), Delacorte Theater, Central Park*

Director Alan Pakula had been impressed by the actor's humor and charisma in *Pirates,* and Meryl Streep, who'd been cast as Sophie, added her vote. In many ways, Nathan was the most difficult role in the film, a paranoid schizophrenic who veered between charm and viciousness. Kline captured Nathan's emotional complexity and added his own athletic grace to the part, particularly in a scene in which he offers a toast atop a railing on the Brooklyn Bridge.

Courtesy of Universal Pictures

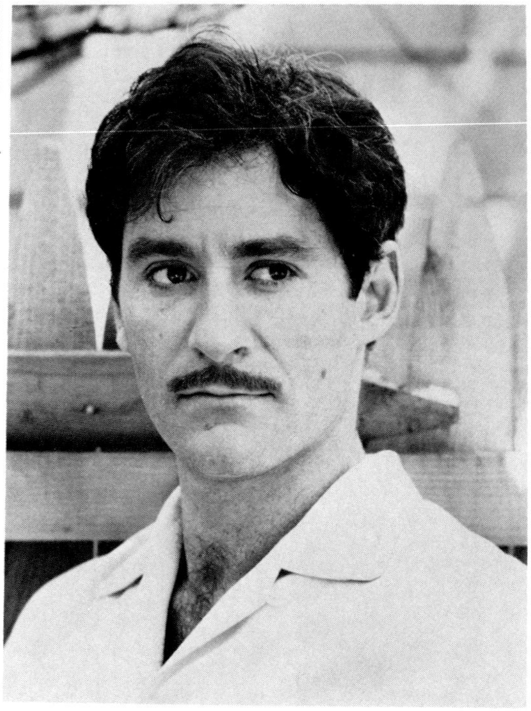

Sophie's Choice *(1982)*

Copyright Susan Cook/Martha Swope Associates

Richard III *(1983), Delacorte Theater, Central Park*

"KEVIN KLINE, IN AN AUSPICIOUS MOVIE DEBUT, CAPTURES THE SCHIZOID GLAMOUR OF NATHAN, WHO IS BOTH ROMANTIC AND RAVAGED. HE CAN PULL THE HAIR-TRIGGER SWITCH BETWEEN NATHAN'S SPRITZY CHARM AND HUMOR AND THE SCARY VIOLENCE OF HIS ANGER."

—Jack Kroll,
Newsweek

"IN HIS FIRST MAJOR VENTURE INTO SHAKESPEARE, KEVIN KLINE PROVES—AND IT'S NO SURPRISE—THAT HE COULD BECOME ONE OF THE BEST CLASSICAL ACTORS OF HIS GENERATION. AS RICHARD III, HE MUST CONTEND WITH A HUMP AND THE SECOND LONGEST ROLE (AFTER HAMLET) IN THE CANON, BUT HIS ATHLETIC GRACE IS UNFLAGGING AND HIS COMMAND OF THE VERSE IS SURE."

—Frank Rich,
The New York Times

A movie version of *Pirates* lacked the zest of the original, but Kline winningly portrayed a Southern gentleman in *The Big Chill,* a rare chance for him to play a happy contemporary character.

During the following two summers, he tackled a pair of Shakespeare's most daring rulers: *Richard III* (1983) and *Henry V* (1984). Explaining his love for the history plays, Kline told *The New York Times,* "The plays are not only about honor, but about war, chivalry, politics, irony, redemption, and the triumph of the human spirit. . . . I'm as intrigued by the similarities between Richard and Henry as the opposites. They are alike in efficacy. They sure know how to get the job done. They are uncompromising . . . And both of them get the girl."

Kline's majestic performances provided ideal summertime theatergoing. "You can complain about bugs and planes and wind

Copyright © 1983 Columbia Pictures Industries, Inc.

With William Hurt in The Big Chill *(1983)*

and rain," he said of the Delacorte Theater, "but when it works, it's magic. There is something indescribable about performing outdoors."

Joseph Papp is unsurprised at the praise Kline has received for his Shakespearean work. "Kevin has all the attributes of what you would call a nineteenth-century actor—proper bearing, tremendous agility, a sense of style, and a command of language that very few American actors have," he says.

After *Henry V,* Kline made two films back to back: *Violets Are Blue,* a coming-of-age story co-starring Sissy Spacek, and *Silverado,* Lawrence Kasdan's epic sci-fi western. "With movies, it's always take what is offered and taste the wind," he said, adding that he considers his career "very much a work in progress."

Somehow, onstage or on-screen, he always manages to choose something worth watching.

"KEVIN KLINE, SO FRANTIC AND REMOTE IN HIS EARLIER SCREEN APPEARANCES, HAS CALMED DOWN AT LAST AND BECOME A WONDERFUL MOVIE ACTOR. . . . PLAYFUL AND GENEROUS AND LEVEL-HEADED, HE MAKES HAPPINESS SEEM EMINENTLY REASONABLE."

—DAVID DENBY, *New York*

John Lithgow

A psychotic killer, a sweet-natured midwestern banker, a wild Irish sailor, a transsexual football player, a heavyweight boxer, an aspiring English comedian, a fundamentalist minister . . . that's the *short* list of characters created by one multitalented actor named John Lithgow.

After an Oscar-nominated performance as former tight end Roberta Muldoon in *The World According to Garp,* Lithgow suddenly found himself "hot" in Hollywood circles at the age of thirty-seven. He'd already spent a decade displaying his versatility on Broadway, beginning with his Tony award–winning work in David Storey's *The Changing Room.*

"Everything that's happened to me as an actor, I never expected to happen," he says with characteristic modesty. "I thought I was going to have a life of doing repertory theater, which was the way I grew up."

Indeed, Lithgow got an early start in professional acting thanks to his father, a producer of Shakespeare festivals in the Midwest. (Young John debuted at age six with a walk-on role in *Henry VI, Part III.*) "My father had a real commitment to doing fine Shakespeare," he recalls. "I owe him a tremendous debt of gratitude—people who grow up in a theater family have an enormous head start professionally."

After graduating from Harvard in 1967, Lithgow went to England on a Fulbright fellowship for two years of study at the London Academy of Music and Dramatic Art, the Royal Shakespeare Company, and the Royal Court Theater. "I didn't want to just jump into New York," he says. "I wanted to continue training because I knew what a discipline acting was."

The Changing Room, a behind-the-scenes look at a British rugby team, proved that John Lithgow was ready for New York. His

"LITHGOW TURNS THE BOASTFUL BLATHERING OF THE SUPERSTITIOUS, PRIMITIVE STOKER INTO THE ULTIMATE DIONYSIAC DANCE OF THE STAGE IRISHMAN. THIS MAKES MAT SOMEWHAT MORE MINDLESS THAN HE REALLY IS, BUT IT GIVES THE PLAY ADDED COLOR AND DRIVE, AND LITHGOW DOES IT WITH NEARLY EPIC ENERGY."

—JACK KROLL, *Newsweek*

With Liv Ullmann in Anna Christie *(1977), Imperial Theatre, New York*

work stood out among the ensemble, earning him a Tony award for his Broadway debut performance.

Through the seventies, he continued to draw praise for his work with the Phoenix Theater Company and his Broadway appearances in *Comedians, My Fat Friend, Anna Christie,* and *Once in a Lifetime.* The latter two plays showed Lithgow equally at ease handling the dark passions of O'Neill and the frothy comedy of Kaufman and Hart. He was particularly fine in *Once in a Lifetime* as a sweet dimwit who adored pistachios and ended up practically running a movie studio. Jokes Lithgow, "I seem to have a peculiar ability to drain all my smarts out. I've played so many parts that are slightly slow-witted, it's kind of my own self-image."

Copyright Van Williams

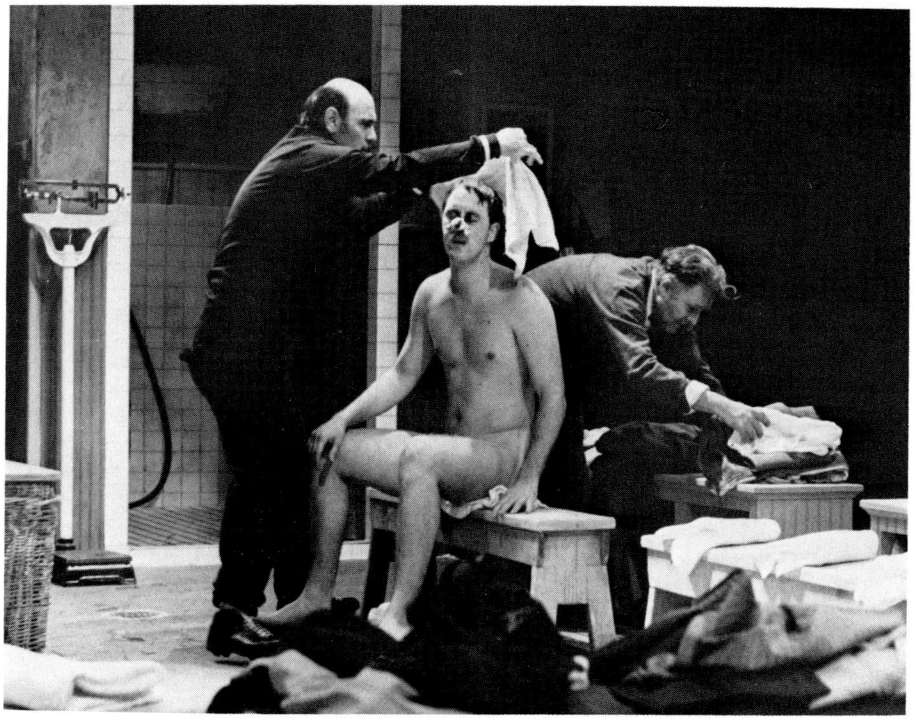

With John Braden and Louis Beachner in The Changing Room *(1973), Morosco Theatre, New York*

"THE PERFORMANCES BELONG TO THE KALEIDOSCOPE AND ARE SCARCELY TO BE ISOLATED FROM ONE ANOTHER, THOUGH MENTION MIGHT POSSIBLY BE MADE OF JOHN LITHGOW'S GLAZED AND BROKEN FORWARD."

—WALTER KERR,
The New York Times

Along the way, he also appeared in a handful of feature films, including *Obsession* (1976), *The Big Fix* (1978), *Rich Kids* (1979), and *All That Jazz* (1980). Working in the movies had never been a goal, he says: "I really thought I was the wrong kind of actor for it. It was totally outside my experience."

But with talent like Lithgow's, success in any medium was practically inevitable. After a chilling performance as a political

Copyright © 1978 Marianne Barcellona

With Max Wright in Once in a Lifetime *(1978), Circle in the Square Theatre, New York*

"THE BEST WORK IN THE LARGE CAST COMES FROM JOHN LITHGOW AS THE SIMPLETON WHO, IN HOLLYWOOD, IS CROWNED PHILOSOPHER-KING. LITHGOW HAS JUST THE RIGHT MIXTURE OF STUPIDITY AND HUMANITY, SHORTCHANGING NEITHER THE IDIOCY NOR THE UNIVERSALITY OF THE CHARACTER."

—JOHN SIMON,
New York

Copyright © 1984 Martha Swope

With Jeffrey DeMunn in Comedians *(1976), Music Box Theatre, New York*

assassin in Brian De Palma's *Blow Out,* he took on the endearing role of Roberta in *The World According to Garp.*

"We did a screen test," says *Garp* director George Roy Hill, "and he had a sympathetic and gentle air about him. Although he had played villains, he came across as a nice person, and I wanted that quality in Roberta."

After the movie was released, Lithgow described his "bizarre adventure" in a thoughtful essay for *Mademoiselle:* "I ended up

"THE PRODUCTION BRILLIANTLY BRIDGES THE GAP BETWEEN PERFORMERS AND AUDIENCES THROUGH [MIKE] NICHOLS'S IRIDESCENT STAGING. COMPELLING PERFORMANCES BY MILO O'SHEA, JONATHAN PRYCE, AND JOHN LITHGOW ROUND OUT A TRIUMPH."

—CHRISOPHER SHARP,
Women's Wear Daily

Copyright © 1981 Viscount Associates

With Nancy Allen in Blow Out *(1981)*

almost inadvertently plumbing the depths of my sexual nature: Sitting alone in my trailer, all dressed up in drag, I would run my hands over the strange, artificial curves of my body, look at myself in the mirror, smile, and wink. Boy-John and girl-John were sharing a secret, sexy joke that no one else was in on. . . . Peeping out from inside this wonderful character, I saw the world of men and women a little differently."

Lithgow's Academy Award nomination for *Garp* (in the same year, ironically, as Dustin Hoffman's for *Tootsie* and Julie Andrews's for *Victor/Victoria*) ushered in two years of almost constant work. During May of 1983 alone, he shot two films—*Footloose* and *Terms of Endearment.* A year later, he was back at the Oscars, nominated for his role as the shy banker who woos Debra Winger in *Terms*—a role that took only five days of shooting. (He lost the award to Jack Nicholson.) Lithgow later remarked that his nomination came because *Terms of Endearment* was a "bigger deal" than *Twilight Zone—The Movie,* in which he stole the show as a crazed airline passenger.

"AS AN UNHINGED AGENT OF EXECUTIVE EVIL, JOHN LITHGOW IS A STUDY IN BLANK-FACED, MONOTONE MENACE—THE G. GORDON LIDDY OF A LIBERAL'S NIGHTMARES."

—RICHARD CORLISS, *Time*

Sandwiched between screen roles as a mad scientist in *The Adventures of Buckaroo Banzai,* an astronaut in *2010,* a police detective in *The Glitter Dome* (for HBO), and a threatened husband in *Mesmerized,* the actor stopped off at the Long Wharf Theater in January 1984 to play the aging boxer in Rod Serling's *Requiem for a Heavyweight.* It was, he says, "the most exciting acting job I've ever had in the theater. You really do see this character come apart before your very eyes and slowly put himself

Copyright Jean Pierre Laffont/Sygma

The World According to Garp *(1982)*

"JOHN LITHGOW IS EXTREMELY TOUCHING AS ROBERTA MULDOON, THE EX–FOOTBALL STAR WHO IS NOW AN OVERSIZED BUT REASONABLY FEMININE TRANSSEXUAL."

—Kathleen Carroll,
New York *Daily News*

Copyright © 1983 Paramount Pictures Corporation

With Debra Winger in Terms of Endearment *(1983)*

"IN ONLY A FEW SCENES, JOHN LITHGOW BRINGS HIS MOONING, OPENHEARTED IOWA ADULTERER TO DELIGHTFUL LIFE."

—DAVID ANSEN,
Newsweek

back together again." Lithgow received glowing reviews in a 1985 Broadway production of *Requiem,* but the play itself was panned and closed quickly.

"John was my first choice," says Long Wharf artistic director Arvin Brown, who first worked with Lithgow more than a decade ago. "I've seen him play inarticulate men, men of somewhat limited intelligence, and I knew he could do it without

Copyright Liaison

The Adventures of Buckaroo Banzai *(1984)*

"MOSTLY, I LAUGHED AT JOHN LITHGOW, WHO BRINGS THE MOVIE THE ANCHOR IT NEEDS. IT'S A GREAT RELIEF TO SEE HIM BEING A SCURVY NUT CASE AFTER HIS GOD-AWFUL SINCERITY IN *FOOTLOOSE.* HE'S AMAZING HERE. . . . HIS SCENES CAN MAKE YOU CRAZY WITH HAPPINESS."

—PAULINE KAEL,
The New Yorker

condescension. His warmth and strength and genuineness all fed the character."

Brown finds Lithgow's success particularly gratifying. "When it occasionally happens that a superb character actor like John becomes a star, it's usually much longer lasting than the kind of stardom that comes with sex imagery," the director says. "I think that John Lithgow is going to be a major American actor for years to come."

Lithgow's commitment to the theater is complicated by the fact that he now lives in Los Angeles with his wife, a UCLA professor, and family. "Working on the stage is important to me," he says. "It gets progressively more difficult the more you act in movies because there's much, much more money in films. As you grow older, those things become persuasive reasons to turn your back on the theater for years on end."

Arvin Brown doesn't expect that to happen with John Lithgow. "When he tackles a part like *Requiem,* he's doing something that will stretch him from head to toe every performance he gives," Brown says. "Once you've known the exhilaration of that, and you're serious about your work, you don't want to escape it for any long period of time. John shows no signs of letting it slip away."

"AN ACTOR WHO HAS OFTEN DONE HIS BEST WORK PLAYING ATHLETES, MR. LITHGOW IS A SEETHING FIGURE OF BRUISED FLESH AND WOUNDED PRIDE IN THE ROLE OF SERLING'S PUGILIST, HARLAN 'MOUNTAIN' MCCLINTOCK. . . . THE PROTAGONIST'S WARMTH EMERGES GRADUALLY, NOT SLOBBERINGLY, IN THIS METICULOUS PERFORMANCE."

—FRANK RICH,
The New York Times

Requiem for a Heavyweight *(1985), Martin Beck Theatre, New York*

Copyright © 1984 Gerry Goodstein

John Malkovich

After only one year in New York, John Malkovich had become one of the country's most acclaimed young actors. But his dues had already been fully paid; before *People, New York,* and *Esquire* asked for interviews, he had spent seven years earning five thousand dollars or less a year as an actor, director, and producer in Chicago.

Malkovich was among nine original members of the Steppenwolf Theatre Company, which began in a parochial-school basement in the summer of 1976 just after most of the nine had graduated from Illinois State University.

"None of us really knew John well," says Terry Kinney, artistic director of Steppenwolf. They'd heard of him, though, both for his unusual taste in clothes (capes, tennis outfits, business suits) and his handling of a bit part in a campus production of *The Man Who Came to Dinner* (he played it as a madman). "We knew he was strange," says Kinney, "and after *Man Who Came to Dinner,* we were pretty much convinced that he was strange and couldn't act." They became more enthusiastic after seeing Malkovich's magnetism on display in another campus play, Harold Pinter's *The Lover.*

For three years after Steppenwolf was formed, the young members supported themselves entirely through outside jobs (Malkovich drove a school bus and sold office supplies). Meanwhile, the company staged five or six plays a season in true ensemble style, with everyone pitching in to build sets, sew costumes, and sell tickets. "We didn't consider ourselves nervy at all," Malkovich says. "Starting a theater was simply our way to do the work that we wanted to do."

The actors supplemented their income further by hiring themselves out as a group for larger productions. In 1979, for example, they worked with New York actor-director Austin

"MALKOVICH PLAYS [LENNIE] WITH APPEALING IDIOCY. THERE IS NO DELIBERATE MENACE, ONLY CONGENIAL RETARDATION, AND TO WATCH HIM LISTEN TO GEORGE'S DREAM OF A PIECE OF LAND TO CALL THEIR OWN IS TO WISH HIM ALL THE PROTECTION HE CAN GET. . . . THIS ROLE IS A NATURAL FOR MALKOVICH AND HIS PORTRAYAL IS YET ANOTHER CHAPTER IN A CAREER THAT SHOULD BE ATTRACTING ATTENTION AROUND THE NATION."

—GLENNA SYSE,
Chicago Sun-Times

With Gary Sinise in Of Mice and Men *(1981), Steppenwolf Theatre, Chicago*

Copyright Lisa Ebright

With Moira Harris in Big Mother *(1981), Steppenwolf Theatre, Chicago*

Pendleton on the Chicago premiere of *Say Goodnight, Gracie,* an Off-Broadway hit comedy about turning thirty. "It was like I opened the door of a closet in the Midwest and found the most exciting young actors I'd ever seen," Pendleton says.

Malkovich played a compulsive wisecracker in *Gracie,* an appropriate part for a person with "a lethal sense of humor," as Pendleton puts it. "There's something completely authentic and unvarnished and undomesticated about his acting," the director says. "Everything he does comes from a deep source that's very private and that he alone understands. It isn't processed through his idea of what other people would want to see."

At the same time that Malkovich was playing roles like Lennie in *Of Mice and Men,* a suburban husband in the satiı ical *Big Mother,* and Tom in *The Glass Menagerie* (the part that he says meant the most to him), he was also building a fine reputation as a director. His freewheeling staging of Lanford Wilson's *Balm in Gilead* won six 1980 Joseph Jefferson awards—Chicago's Tony—including best director.

"*BIG MOTHER,* THE LATEST LATE-NIGHT, GROSS-OUT SHOW AT STEPPENWOLF THEATER, IS DUMB, VULGAR, CRASS, DISGUSTING, AND, FOR ABOUT HALF OF ITS 40 MINUTES, EXCRUCIATINGLY FUNNY. . . . THE CAST WAS TERRIFIC . . . [INCLUDING] JOHN MALKOVICH, IN PENCIL MUSTACHE AND SHINY BLACK WIG, AS THE VORACIOUS HUSBAND."

—RICHARD CHRISTIANSEN,
Chicago Tribune

"I think John is the best young director in America," says Pendleton. "When I directed *Loose Ends* at Steppenwolf in 1981, there was one scene I just couldn't crack. He went out with me to a coffee shop until two in the morning and conducted this Socratic dialogue which finally led me to the heart of the scene. I've never talked to another director who was able to be so concrete and specific."

Malkovich's next Steppenwolf role turned out to be the one that changed his life: Lee, the desert-rat brother in Sam Shepard's *True West.* Gary Sinise's electric production gave new life to a play that had been badly staged in New York, and Malkovich's hilarious yet creepy performance earned him the 1982 Jefferson Award for best actor.

When producer Wayne Adams, a fan of Steppenwolf since 1979, offered to bring *True West* to New York, panic ensued within the company. "They'd call me and say, 'We can't do this; it'll ruin everything,' " Pendleton recalls. "And I said, 'Listen, guys, you can't keep this from the world forever.' "

Recalls Adams, "I told John, 'If you come to New York and we do this really well, everyone, including television and film people, is going to see it. Things are going to happen real fast, kiddo.' "

The producer was right: The New York critics compared Malkovich to Jack Nicholson and Marlon Brando, he won the 1983 Clarence Derwent Award for most promising male actor, and yes, *everyone* came to see *True West.*

"I thought he was brilliant," says film director Robert Benton, who immediately thought of casting the young actor in *Places in the Heart.* "I called him in, and then I said to a friend who shall go nameless, 'I'm talking to Malkovich about this picture.' And the guy said, 'Did you see *True West*? That guy's gotta be psychotic.' And I said, 'A psychotic might sustain that for about a minute and a half, but he couldn't sustain it for a whole performance night after night.' When John came in, he was this soft-spoken person, exactly right for the part."

Malkovich, who had never aspired to movie stardom—or stardom of *any* kind—soon found himself being called "the best thing to happen to screen acting in a long while" (Janet Maslin, *The New York Times*). As Mr. Will, the blind boarder in *Places in the Heart,* he was touching yet never maudlin. In *The Killing Fields,* he gave a forceful performance as a news photographer in Cambodia, prompting Maslin to suggest that the movie would have been even better with him in the lead.

Copyright © 1984 Tri-Star Pictures

Places in the Heart *(1984)*

"THE EDGY PRECISION OF MALKOVICH'S MANNER, THE VERY COCK OF HIS HEAD AS HE LISTENS FOR CLUES TO THE REALITY HE CANNOT SEE, ARE THE CONTRIBUTIONS OF ANOTHER FINE ACTOR."

—RICHARD SCHICKEL,
Time

Copyright © 1984 Martha Swope

With Sam Schacht in True West *(1982), Cherry Lane Theatre, New York*

"IT IS MR. MALKOVICH, IN THE MORE FLAMBOYANT ROLE, WHO AMBLES AWAY WITH THE EVENING'S ACTING TROPHY. WITH HIS AIR OF FEIGNED CONFIDENTIALITY AND AFFECTING A SLIGHT LISP, HE SOUNDS A BIT LIKE JACK NICHOLSON AT HIS WILIEST, AND IN COMMON WITH ROBERT DUVALL, HE OFFERS A THREAT OF IMMINENT EXPLOSIVENESS. HOWEVER, THE PERFORMANCE IS A COMIC ORIGINAL. WITH PERFECT TIMING AND INEXHAUSTIBLE EXPRESSIVENESS, HE IS AMUSING AND MENACING AT THE SAME INSTANT . . . AN ACTING HOLE-IN-ONE."

—MEL GUSSOW,
The New York Times

Copyright Inge Morath/Magnum Photos Inc.

With Kate Reid, Dustin Hoffman, and Stephen Lang in Death of a Salesman *(1984), Broadhurst Theatre, New York*

"MR. MALKOVICH, HULKING AND UNSMILING, IS AN INVERSION OF MR. HOFFMAN'S FATHER. ANYONE WHO SAW THIS REMARKABLE YOUNG ACTOR AS THE RAMBUNCTIOUS RASCAL OF *TRUE WEST* MAY FIND HIS TRANSFORMATION HERE AS ASTONISHING AS THE STAR'S. HIS BIFF IS SOFT AND TENTATIVE, WITH SULLEN EYES AND A SLOW, DISTANT VOICE THAT SEEMS ENTOMBED WITH HIS ABORTED TEENAGE PROMISE."

—FRANK RICH,
The New York Times

Copyright © 1984 Goldcrest Films and Television Ltd.

The Killing Fields *(1984)*

"JOHN MALKOVICH, WHO SEEMS DESTINED TO BECOME ONE OF THE FINEST AMERICAN CHARACTER ACTORS, GIVES A FORCEFUL PERFORMANCE AS A DARING COMBAT PHOTOGRAPHER WHO SUSTAINS HIMSELF ON DRUGS."

—KATHLEEN CARROLL,
New York *Daily News*

After shooting both movies, Malkovich returned to the stage in a very different play, *Death of a Salesman,* and gave a new interpretation of Biff Loman. His Biff was withdrawn and depressed, a striking contrast to the feisty Willy Loman of Dustin Hoffman. Though Malkovich had played Biff at Steppenwolf in 1980, he continues to call it his most challenging part.

Just after *Salesman* opened on Broadway to raves and capacity business, Malkovich made his New York directing debut with *Balm in Gilead,* a joint production using actors from both Steppenwolf and Circle Repertory Company. The spectacle of twenty-nine actors onstage together, their lines overlapping, their movements choreographed to the beat of Bruce Springsteen music, was terrifically exciting to watch.

Malkovich then traveled to Europe to star in the film version of Nicholas Gage's *Eleni* opposite Kate Nelligan. Yet his newfound fame, including an Oscar nomination for *Places in the Heart,* hasn't changed his priorities—the stage is still number one. "Theater gives me the opportunity to do things of substance," he says. "It doesn't have to be watered down or geared to mass commercial acceptance."

Directing a new play at Steppenwolf was first on Malkovich's agenda for 1985. "John hasn't changed a bit," notes Terry Kinney. "He's always been eccentric, he's always said what's on his mind, and he was never in awe of anyone. He mixes with a whole new set of people now, and yet we're all very confident that we're his real home."

"John has always been a man who knows what he likes," says Austin Pendleton, "and he can't be talked into anything he doesn't like. I really think that he will handle success with the ease of someone who didn't need it that much to begin with."

Mandy Patinkin

Power, passion, conviction, daring—the larger-than-life qualities Mandy Patinkin displays in his acting inspire equally fervent responses. Sidney Lumet, his director in the movie *Daniel,* calls him "a bolt of lightning"; producer Joseph Papp says he has "the power to play King Lear"; director Harold Prince says his energy "changed the balance of everything" in the American production of *Evita.*

Add in good looks and a gorgeous two-octave tenor voice, and Mandy Patinkin, thirty-two, emerges as a formidable young leading man. Like many of his peers, however, Patinkin seems genuinely to care more about the quality of the projects he does than about personal recognition.

"I can't be alive if I'm doing things I don't believe in," he said when *Daniel* was released in 1983. Only half the critics shared his feelings about that particular film (a fictionalized account of the espionage trial and execution of the Rosenbergs), but Patinkin's ability to commit himself so fully to his work paid off in the cases of Barbra Streisand's *Yentl* and Stephen Sondheim's Broadway musical *Sunday in the Park with George.* Playing Georges Seurat in *Sunday in the Park* "was one of the richest experiences of my life," he says, well worth the four months of development he devoted to it.

This quintessential New York actor was actually born and raised in Chicago, where he discovered performing at a neighborhood youth center. After attending the University of Kansas for two years, he transferred to the drama division at Juilliard in 1972. Finding the intense pressure and grueling schedule intolerable, he quit two years later, before completing his degree.

Within a year, however, Patinkin began working at Joseph Papp's Public Theater. He played Mary Beth Hurt's fiancé in

"PATINKIN, AN ANTIC GNOME OF A CHE, WALTZES HIS WAY THROUGH THE MUSICAL WITH WHIPLASH IMAGES AND A REAL SENSE OF GUT-EATING AGONY COMBINED WITH A DETACHED AMUSEMENT."

—CLIVE BARNES, *New York Post*

With Patti LuPone in Evita *(1979), Broadway Theatre, New York*

Trelawny of the Wells (in a cast including Meryl Streep and John Lithgow) in 1975, Fortinbras in *Hamlet* (1975), and a gay Union soldier with Peter Weller in *Rebel Women* (1976). At the Off-Broadway Hudson Guild Theater, he won admiring reviews as a third-world guerrilla leader in Christopher Hampton's *Savages* (1977). Several months later, he made his Broadway debut as the young lover of a cancer victim in the Pulitzer Prize–winning *Shadow Box*.

Patinkin then did a series of bit parts in movies, playing a swimming-pool cleaner in *The Big Fix* (1976), a *Wall Street Journal* reporter in *The Last Embrace* (1979), and a Puerto Rican cabdriver in *Night of the Juggler* (1980). He made a brief foray into

Copyright Diane Gorodnitzki

With Anita Grumish in Royal Gambit *(1974), Juilliard School, New York*

TV comedy with *That Thing on ABC,* a special that aired in January 1978 and was designed to compete with *Saturday Night Live*. (The network decided not to pursue the show.) "I'm just a joker," he says, "but everything I've done that got attention was serious."

Laughs were indeed few in *Evita,* the smash-hit Broadway musical featuring Patinkin's charismatic performance as Che Guevara. According to director Harold Prince, the London Che had been "a sort of Lord Byronesque figure—very fragile and poetical. The character observed the activity and commented on it. When we came to New York, Mandy was one of the last people we saw, and we gave him the job knowing that he would not be at all in the same mold. He became the motor of the show, the driving

"PATINKIN IS HAVING A FIELD DAY WITH THE REVOLUTIONARY. A FAST-DEVELOPING ACTOR OF TECHNIQUE, VERSATILITY, INTELLIGENCE, AND DRIVE, HE TAKES THE CHARACTER'S CONTRADICTIONS (INTELLECTUALISM, MILITANCE, MONEY, REBELLION, DECENCY, BRUTALITY) AND WORKS THEM INTO A BOLD AND MEMORABLE CHARACTERIZATION."

—MARTIN GOTTFRIED, *New York Post*

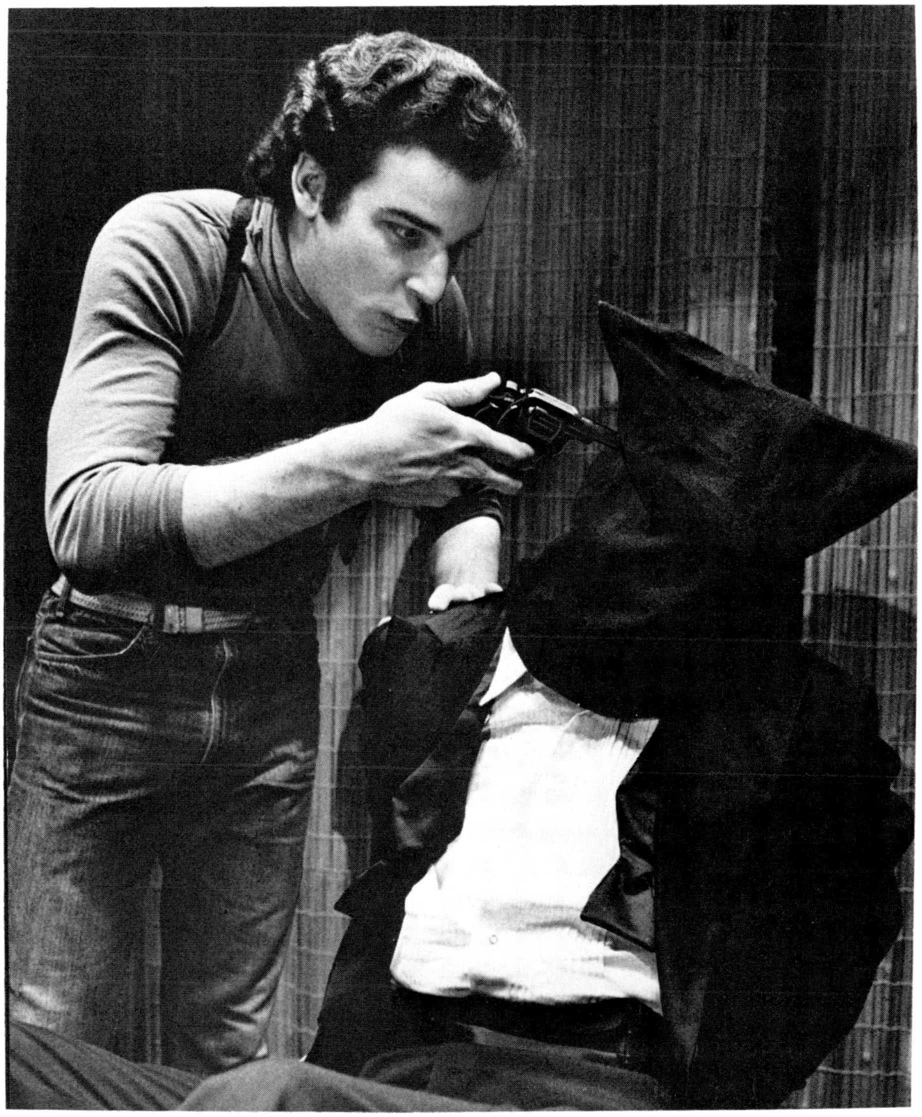

Charles Marinaro

Savages *(1977), Hudson Guild Theater, New York*

Copyright © 1984 Martha Swope Associates/Susan Cook

Henry IV, Part I *(1981), Delacorte Theater, Central Park*

force, and that worked out wonderfully."

Just after Patinkin picked up a Tony Award for *Evita,* film director Milos Forman cast him as Tateh, the Russian immigrant and silhouette artist who becomes a movie director in *Ragtime.* Though he appeared in only a few scenes, Patinkin was singled out by reviewers for his striking characterization.

Back onstage in the Public Theater's 1981 Central Park production of *Henry IV, Part I,* he drew mixed reviews for his work as Hotspur. Some critics found him too malicious, but Joseph Papp praises the "deep conviction" he brings to every role. "His acting is risky, it's erratic, and it's provocative," says Papp. "He has a commitment that becomes so powerful, it makes you believe him."

Sidney Lumet's 1983 film *Daniel* was marked by deeply felt performances from Patinkin and Lindsay Crouse. In spite of them and the publicity generated by ongoing arguments about the guilt of the Rosenbergs, the movie failed to attract large audiences. *Yentl,* released three months later, met a happier fate. Even critics who disliked Barbra Streisand's sweeping story of a Hasidic girl's desire to learn, admired Patinkin's work as Avigdor. His charm and youthful intensity made it easy to see why the character Yentl would become enamored with him.

"MANDY PATINKIN PLAYS THE INTEMPERATE HOTSPUR WITH THE RASH ÉLAN CENTRAL TO THE CHARACTER. HE IS MOST HUMOROUSLY ADEPT IN HIS SARCASTIC LACING OF EFFETE COURTLINESS; YET THERE ARE TOO MANY MOMENTS WHEN HIS MAIN CONCERN SEEMS TO BE GETTING HIS SPEECHES OVER WITH."

—Don Nelsen,
New York *Daily News*

Copyright © 1984 David McGough/DMI

Ragtime *(1981)*

"AMONG THE MORE MEMORABLE SEQUENCES IS ONE IN WHICH A JEWISH IMMIGRANT (PLAYED BY THE UNUSUALLY CHARISMATIC MANDY PATINKIN) TOSSES HIS ADULTEROUS WIFE OUT OF THEIR TENEMENT FLAT IN A SWIFTLY PACED, ARTFULLY CHOREOGRAPHED ACTION SEQUENCE."

—KATHLEEN CARROLL,
New York *Daily News*

At that point, Patinkin could have chosen from any number of movie offers but he already had a challenging project lined up in *Sunday in the Park with George.* After spending the summer of 1983 perfecting the first act of the play at Off-Broadway's Playwrights Horizons, Patinkin, Bernadette Peters, composer Stephen Sondheim, and director-writer James Lapine regrouped in February 1984 to ready the show for Broadway. During previews two songs were dropped, two were added, and the entire second act was reworked. The musical opened to great acclaim, and both stars received Tony nominations.

For Patinkin, *Sunday in the Park*'s exploration of creativity reflected many of his own feelings about stage acting. "I love the line at the end of the play about 'so many possibilities,' " he says. "In the theater, the longer you stay, the more possibilities you can search out. You can do that in film, but when you decide that things are good and it's what you need, you go on. But it could be a thousand other things, too. You want to live it again."

Seurat, though fascinating, is a humorless character, so Patinkin eagerly accepted the role of Glenn Close's husband in the comedy

"MANDY PATINKIN GIVES A MIRACULOUS PERFORMANCE AS PAUL. BRAWNY AND VIRILE, PATINKIN, WHO HAS VALENTINO EYES, WORKS UP A STORM OF JOYOUS LIFE, TURNING THE SHABBY APARTMENT INTO A THEATER AS HE HOLDS HIS CHILDREN ALOFT IN TRIUMPH."

—David Denby,
New York

"MANDY PATINKIN SIZZLES WITH SCHOLARLY AND SEXUAL ENERGY AS AVIGDOR."

—Jack Kroll,
Newsweek

Copyright © 1983 Paramount Pictures Corporation

With Lindsay Crouse in Daniel *(1983)*

Copyright © 1983 Ladbroke Entertainments Limited; released by United Artists

With Amy Irving and Barbra Streisand in Yentl *(1983)*

Copyright © 1984 Martha Swope

With William Parry, Cris Groenendaal, and Bernadette Peters in Sunday in the Park with George *(1984), Booth Theatre, New York*

film *Maxie,* which was shot in the fall of 1984. Shedding his heavy beard, the actor got to disclose a playful, romantic side as a mild-mannered librarian who must cope with his wife's possession by the ghost of a flapper. "I was dying for something different," he says. "I just wanted to literally bust out—like Seurat said, 'move on.' "

Patinkin hopes that one of his next moves will be to join with Close, Kevin Kline, and others to do a season of great plays in repertory on Broadway. "We'd all work for low salaries so that people could afford it," he says enthusiastically. "It's been talked about off and on, but I'm quite convinced it will happen. It'll happen . . . and it will be *great.*"

"MR. PATINKIN IS A CRUCIBLE OF INTELLECTUAL FIRE—'HE BURNS YOU WITH HIS EYES,' SAYS DOT, WITH REASON."

—FRANK RICH, *The New York Times*

Pamela Reed

There's nothing actressy about Pamela Reed, who looks like and talks like anybody's next-door neighbor. This makes her all the more believable when she unleashes her sizable talent onstage and in films like *The Right Stuff.*

"Pamela has a kind of earthiness that very few actresses have," says Joseph Papp, who gave Reed her first big break in the Public Theater's 1978 production of Sam Shepard's *Curse of the Starving Class.* "She's very logical, with the kind of good sense and intelligence that has nothing to do with education—she brings it from life."

The daughter of a Laborers' International Union executive, Reed ran a day-care center and worked with Head Start children before deciding to study acting at age twenty-one. She then entered the University of Washington's drama department, paying for her last year of school by working one summer on the Trans-Alaska pipeline. In 1975, without waiting to pick up her diploma, she says, "I just got on a plane and came to New York with sixty dollars in my pocket. Ignorance is bliss."

Reed found work in a couple of Off-Broadway showcases, then detoured into a 1977 television series about newspaper reporters called *The Andros Targets.* "After five weeks, I was praying that it would not continue," she says. "I don't think I realized that I had signed seven years of my life away. I don't have what it takes to play one character for long periods of time." When the show was canceled after thirteen episodes, Reed returned to New York for good.

Soon she began a fruitful association with Joseph Papp, which continues today. Her audition with him for the role of a thirteen-year-old girl in *Curse of the Starving Class* remains a fond memory. "I was never so scared in my entire life," she recalls.

"[DIRECTOR PETER YATES] GETS MARVELOUSLY SUBTLE PERFORMANCES OUT OF HIS GREAT CAST—FOR INSTANCE, THE BEAUTIFULLY TIMED CRESCENDO OF RELIEF AND GRATITUDE WORKED UP BY HURT AND PAMELA REED WHEN THEY REALIZE THEY AREN'T IN LOVE, WERE NEVER IN LOVE, AND NEEDN'T KEEP UP THE PRETENSE OF PASSION ANYMORE."

—DAVID DENBY,
New York

With William Hurt in Eyewitness *(1981)*

Copyright Frederic Ohringer

With Olympia Dukakis in Curse of the Starving Class *(1978), Public Theater, New York*

"PAMELA REED IS FIERCE AND FUNNY AS THE DAUGHTER."

—Richard Eder,
The New York Times

"When I finished, I was sent out of the room while he discussed it with the director. They called me back in and Joe said 'Okay.' I ran to him and threw my arms around him and said, 'I'll never forget this day as long as I live.' And he said, 'I don't think I will, either.' He was so kind."

After playing Helena in Papp's 1978 Central Park production of *All's Well That Ends Well,* Reed won a lead role in *Getting Out,* Marsha Norman's acclaimed first play. She gave a remarkable performance as a vicious teenager imprisoned for robbery and second-degree murder. Her character, Arlie, represented the rebellious past self of a shaky ex-con beautifully acted by the late Susan Kingsley. Together, the two actresses gave a moving portrayal of one woman's road from desperation to hope.

Getting Out director Jon Jory praises Reed's "laserlike concentration, analytical intelligence, and powerful stage energy—she's like a rocket." She, in turn, calls Arlie her favorite and most challenging role.

Reed knows what she likes in a script: "integrity in the through-line of a character [the character behaving consistently through the piece], things that aren't contrived, things that are about something. You don't want people to feel ripped off when they leave the theater. They may feel happy or sad, but you hope they'll be glad they came."

The actress got her start in feature films in 1980 as the notorious madam Belle Starr in *The Long Riders.* The following year she played Paul LeMat's down-to-earth second wife in *Melvin and Howard* and shared a terrific break-up scene with William Hurt in *Eyewitness.*

Though she was seductive as Belle and winning in all three roles, Reed knows she isn't cast for her glamour. "The only time I might ever be wanted for my looks is if somebody wants to do a remake of *Tobacco Road,*" she jokes. "That's not to put myself down—I can pull it together and hold my head up with the best of them. But there are things I don't get because I'm not pretty enough."

Instead, she gets parts because of her range and her ability to play both comedy and drama. In April 1981 she was the ingenue lead in what she calls "the shortest running Neil Simon play," *Fools,* which opened and closed on Broadway in one month. "I've never seen anything like it," she says of the savage criticism given to Simon's story of a Ukrainian town filled with double-talking imbeciles. Yet she found *Fools* a wonderful collaborative experience. "The best writers, like Neil, are the most flexible ones, because there comes a point in the rehearsal process when the actors probably know as much about their character as the writer. If everyone is sensitive to what the play is about, you can come up with great rewrites. Neil was unbelievable about that."

Copyright © 1980 United Artists Corporation

The Long Riders *(1980)*

"THE CASTING AND PERFORMANCE ARE RIGHT AT EVERY LEVEL, WITH FINE SUPPORTING WORK BY PAMELA REED AS THE TIGHT-FEATURED, LIBIDINOUS PROSTITUTE BELLE STARR, WHO SPEAKS IN A WONDERFULLY PURSY MIDWESTERN ACCENT."

—ROGER ANGELL,
The New Yorker

Getting Out *(1979), Theater De Lys, New York*

Copyright © 1984 Martha Swope

"PAMELA REED, HER WIDE-SET EYES AND ROUND FACE GIVING HER A CHILDISH LOOK THAT MAKES HER HELLION ENERGY ALL THE MORE STARTLING, IS GROWLING, SARDONIC, VIOLENT, AND PITIFUL BY TURNS. IT IS A PERFORMANCE THAT IN ITS VARIETY AND FORCE IS TREMENDOUSLY MOVING."

—RICHARD EDER,
The New York Times

Copyright © 1984 Gerry Goodstein

Standing on My Knees *(1982), Manhattan Theatre Club, New York*

"ALL THE UNCONTROLLABLE COMPLEXITIES OF MADNESS ARE IN THIS PERFORMANCE, CONTROLLED. MISS REED TRULY IS TWO PERSONS, EACH PERFECTLY REALIZED AND INEXTRICABLY ENCAPSULATED IN THE OTHER. WE WATCH THIS PERFORMANCE ON *OUR* KNEES."

—John Simon,
New York

Reed's only other Broadway appearance, in a 1978 drama called *The November People,* also ended quickly. "It doesn't matter to me whether a play's in a Broadway house or an Off-Broadway house as long as the project is good," she says. "I just want to do interesting roles and learn my craft."

Both desires were satisfied in *Standing on My Knees,* a case study of schizophrenia staged in the fall of 1982 at the Manhattan Theatre Club. Critics found Reed's portrait of a disturbed yet talented poet riveting. "It was a killer," she says, "but the stuff that demands the most of you also makes you the happiest."

For most of the past two years, Reed has kept busy acting in feature films and TV movies. "I have fallen in love with film," she says, though she says she finds it neither easier nor harder than stage acting: "Something is difficult when the scene doesn't work, not because you're doing it in front of a camera or on the stage."

In *The Right Stuff,* she played the unconventional wife of astronaut Gordon "Gordo" Cooper (Dennis Quaid). Next, she co-starred with Judd Hirsch and Martin Balsam in *The Goodbye People,* a movie about three eccentrics at Coney Island that was never widely released. Her TV work included *Heart of Steel* (1983), an ABC film about the closing of a steel mill, and NBC's *Scandal Sheet* (1985), about a sleazy tabloid newspaper, the latter opposite Burt Lancaster.

Her biggest popular success may come with the 1985 release of *Clan of the Cave Bear,* in which she plays Eza, a Neanderthal medicine woman who finds and raises a Cro-Magnon child. Her daily makeup session for the movie, she reports, took three hours to complete.

In the spring of 1984, Reed also found time to stop by the Public Theater and play four roles—a sadistic stepmother, a pious Baptist, a nine-year-old girl, and a human scarecrow—in *Fen,* Caryl Churchill's drama of poor landworkers in eastern England. The entire ensemble cast won Obie awards for their work that year.

"I like my career," declares the plain-spoken actress. "When I came to New York, I said I wasn't going to do television or film. I didn't even want to do *Broadway* because I thought it was too commercial. Well, I've had the opportunity to do all those things. I have one goal now, and that's to be working when I'm seventy-five. My heroes are Ruth Gordon, Art Carney, Burt Lancaster—people who know their craft and have lasted a long, long time."

Copyright © 1983 The Ladd Company

With Dennis Quaid in The Right Stuff *(1983)*

"THE WOMEN ARE SO STRONG IN THIS MOVIE, YOU WISH THEY HAD EVEN MORE TO DO. BEST OF ALL, PERHAPS, IS PAMELA REED (ONE OF THE FINEST UNSUNG ACTRESSES AROUND) AS GORDO COOPER'S ESTRANGED WIFE, TRUDY, WHO IS FORCED TO MAKE A GOOD SHOW OF THEIR MARRIAGE TO HELP HIM UP THE PYRAMID."

—DAVID ANSEN, *Newsweek*

Copyright © 1984 Martha Swope

With Linda Griffiths and Robin Bartlett in Fen *(1984), Public Theater, New York*

"MISS REED IS BEST KNOWN FOR HER PERFORMANCES AS BOISTEROUS MIDDLE AMERICAN WOMEN. HERE SHE IS JUST AS AUTHENTIC AS THE PATHOLOGICAL YET SYMPATHETIC DICKENSIAN STEPMOTHER OR AS VAL'S FORLORN NINE-YEAR-OLD DAUGHTER, BEGGING FOR LOVE. THIS ACTRESS HAS A PROTEAN RANGE, BUT SHE REVEALS IT THROUGH THE SUBTLEST OF MEANS."

—FRANK RICH, *The New York Times*

Eric Roberts

Eric Roberts is, in the very best sense, a passionate actor. The characters he plays are brimming with emotion, and Roberts, unlike many performers, is willing to make himself unappealing in order to bring them to life. Even the murderer Paul Snider in *Star 80* emerged as a three-dimensional—if repellent—human being. *New Yorker* critic Pauline Kael has described the twenty-nine-year-old Roberts as "probably the most imaginative high flier of the younger actors. He has the audacity to risk going too far for the audience, and maybe even bewildering it."

Roberts grew up in Atlanta and began acting as a child with a local theater company run by his father. Interestingly, he found that memorization controlled his childhood stutter, traces of which can still be heard in conversation. A high-school graduate at age sixteen, he studied for two years at London's Royal Academy of Dramatic Arts, then moved to New York to enter the American Academy. Disappointed with the training there, he quit after a year.

At that point, says Roberts, "I just wanted to work in the theater." And he did, playing small parts in *Rebel Women* at the Public Theater, *A Streetcar Named Desire* at Princeton's McCarter Theater, and *Alms for the Middle Class* at New Haven's Long Wharf Theater.

Three years later, however, in 1978, he became the subject of intense studio hype when he played the title role in *King of the Gypsies,* an overblown epic that flopped at the box office. In a curious way, the movie's failure may have been good for Roberts, allowing him to take on a series of excellent—though smaller-scale—parts, beginning with that of Willa Cather's doomed drifter in *Paul's Case,* on PBS-TV.

He returned to the stage in triumph with *Mass Appeal* (1980), a comedy about the relationship between a rebellious seminarian

"ERIC ROBERTS AS MARK DOES WELL WITH THE TRICKY TASK OF TURNING YOUTHFUL RIGHTEOUSNESS INTO MORAL SWEETNESS."

—JACK KROLL, *Newsweek*

With Milo O'Shea in Mass Appeal *(1980), Manhattan Theatre Club, New York*

Copyright © 1978 Paramount Pictures Corporation

King of the Gypsies *(1978)*

"[DIRECTOR FRANK] PIERSON TAILORS THE WHOLE MOVIE FOR THE MALE-INGENUE PERFORMANCE, AND ROBERTS SEIZES HIS OPPORTUNITY BY THE THROAT. . . . HE MOVES WITH A SCRAMBLING, SPINNING GRACE, AND HE HAS A VAGRANT, DEBONAIR STREAK UNDER THE SURLINESS THAT COULD MAKE HIM EXTREMELY APPEALING IN TIME."

—David Denby,
New York

"ERIC ROBERTS IS A PERFECT PAUL. HIS EYES HAVE THAT 'CERTAIN HYSTERICAL BRILLIANCY' CATHER DESCRIBED; HE IS EXACTLY THE KIND OF PRETTY, WIDE-EYED DILETTANTE WHO, IN 1980, WOULD DRIFT UNNOTICED THROUGH THE UNDERBELLY OF NEW YORK SHOW BUSINESS."

—Frank Rich,
Time

Paul's Case *(PBS-TV, 1980)*

Copyright © 1984 Ken Howard

Courtesy of Universal Pictures

With Sissy Spacek in Raggedy Man *(1981)*

"IN A BREATHTAKING SEDUCTION SCENE, [ROBERTS] MAKES NITA A GIFT OF RAYONS . . . GLOVES HER HAND WITH HIS PRESENT, CARESSES THE HAND, CLENCHES IT, AND LIFTS HER UP IN A KISS ACCOMPANIED BY BENNY GOODMAN'S 'THE LADY'S IN LOVE WITH YOU' THAT TURNS INTO A FOXTROT THAT LEADS TO BED. HIS TIMING IS EXQUISITE."

—CARRIE RICKEY,
The Village Voice

Copyright Steve Vaugh/Sygma

Star 80 *(1983)*

and a complacent parish priest. Roberts gave an affecting performance, full of feeling, without becoming strident—a perfect balance for co-star Milo O'Shea's exuberance.

His next feature film was *Raggedy Man,* a romantic story set in rural Texas during World War II. "I'd love to find another Teddy," he says of his character, a sweet-natured sailor who wooed Sissy Spacek. Another impressive PBS project, a remake of Nathanael West's *Miss Lonelyhearts,* followed in 1982, with Roberts starring as a tormented advice columnist.

The release of *Raggedy Man* should have coincided with Eric Roberts's Broadway debut in a second production of *Mass Appeal,* but a disagreement with the director caused him to drop out. He was also recuperating from an automobile accident in which he had suffered injuries to his face, broken both ankles, and which had left him in a coma for three days. Soon, however, his biggest acting challenge presented itself: *Star 80.*

"I like stories about people who come from behind," Roberts says. "I'm in love with the American dream." So was Paul Snider, the hustler husband of *Playboy* centerfold Dorothy Stratten, but Snider lacked the talent and temperament to make the dream come true. Playing him, Roberts transformed himself into a frighteningly unstable loser—perhaps *too* frightening for many critics and moviegoers.

"IT IS REALLY ERIC ROBERTS WHO GIVES THIS FILM ITS CENTRIFRUGAL FORCE. PUMPING HIS MUSCLES FOR SUPERIORITY, BELLOWING TO HIDE HIS FEAR, SWEATING AMBITION AND DROOLING WITH INSINCERE CHARM, HE LITERALLY SWALLOWS THE SCREEN WITH THE RANGE AND FLUIDITY OF HIS CHARACTERIZATION."

—REX REED,
New York Post

Lanny Nagler

With Jan Miner in The Glass Menagerie *(1983), Hartford Stage Company, Hartford, Connecticut*

"ERIC ROBERTS AS TOM, THE DUTIFUL SON, IS POWERFUL. THE SCENE IN WHICH HIS ANGER AND FRUSTRATION BECAUSE OF HIS MOTHER'S INABILITY TO FACE REALITY BOILS OVER INTO SHOUTING FURY WAS UNUSUALLY EFFECTIVE, AS WAS HIS PORTRAYAL OF THE DRUNKENNESS THAT FOLLOWED."

—R. C. HAMMERICH,
The Morning Union, Springfield, Mass.

At first, director Bob Fosse didn't think Roberts was right for the part—he had seen the actor's gentle performance in *Raggedy Man*—but an excellent audition and a look at *Miss Lonelyhearts* changed his mind. "Eric had the same kind of likability that Montgomery Clift did in *A Place in the Sun,*" he says. "Somehow, no matter how evil and sleazy the *Star 80* character was, I sympathized with him."

Fosse, a master of both theater and film, says that Roberts and Mariel Hemingway rehearsed together a full six weeks before shooting began. "We blocked out all the scenes, taped the floor, and had run-throughs just like a play," he says. "Eric loved that, of course, because that was the way he was used to working. He's a real director's actor—there isn't anything you ask of him that he wouldn't try to do. I was very disappointed that he didn't get an Academy Award nomination for *Star 80,* because I think he gave an extraordinary performance."

In the end, the film received equal measures of praise and criticism, but the public stayed away. Says Roberts, "The only thing I regret about *Star 80* is that Bob Fosse's work was not recognized. It was a horrible story but a fantastic film. I didn't get hurt by it, and God knows, just working for Fosse does a lot for anybody. I think he's a genius."

Immediately after finishing *Star 80,* Roberts went to Hartford, Connecticut, to play Tom in a special memorial production of

Tennessee Williams's *The Glass Menagerie.* "When he gave that final speech, there wasn't a dry eye in the house," says director George Keathley. "Eric is a brilliant actor with a wonderful way of making any part his own."

Back in New York, Roberts joined Mickey Rourke in Little Italy to play what he calls "a different kind of lunatic" in *The Pope of Greenwich Village.* Though the movie included a funny, quirky performance from Roberts as a bumbling thief, and a silky one from Rourke as his cousin, it didn't become an enormous hit.

Throughout his career, Roberts has staunchly referred to himself as a character actor. "That's because I believe that charactor actors can work until the walls come tumbling down," he says. "There are very few people who can play leads for more than twelve years. You have to get ready to bend."

As for the stage, "If they'd stop doing revivals and casting successful plays with nothing but movie stars so they can sell tickets, I would do more," says Eric Roberts—passionately.

With Mickey Rourke in The Pope of Greenwich Village *(1984)*

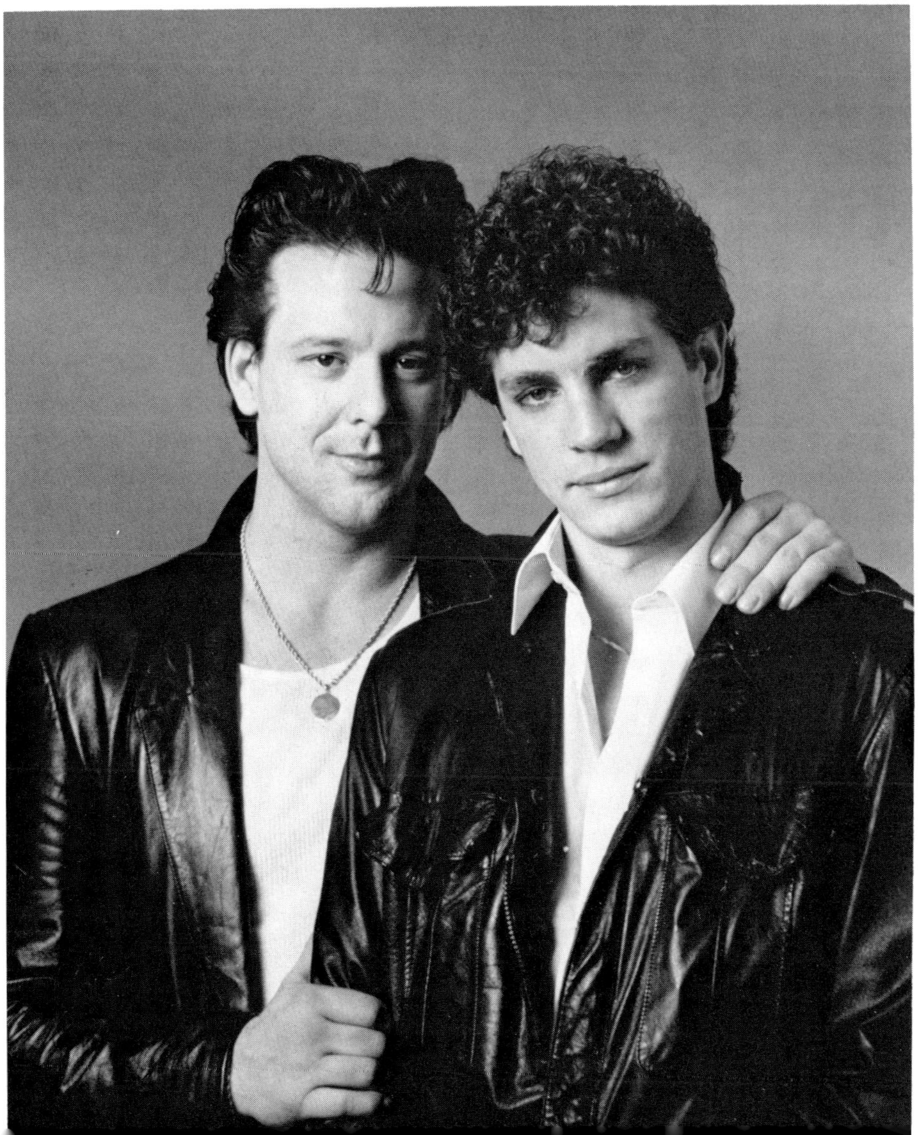

Copyright Barbra Walz/Outline; released by United Artists

"ERIC ROBERTS'S WEIRD, OUT-AT-THE-EDGE PERFORMANCE GIVES THE PICTURE WHATEVER DRIVE AND POINT IT HAS. ROBERTS DOMINATES THE FILM . . . HE GOES WAY PAST REALISM INTO A STYLIZED, EXAGGERATED CLOWNING."

—PAULINE KAEL,
The New Yorker

NO DOMESTIC
COMEDIES

John Shea

John Shea's boyish handsomeness and charm make him a natural screen heartthrob. But Shea, who won international recognition for his work in the 1982 film *Missing,* has never left the theater for long. "The stage provides a return to your emotional foundations," he says. "You're constantly testing yourself. An actor is only as good as the roles he plays—it's that simple." In Shea's case, those roles have often been in ensemble pieces rather than star vehicles, and that's the way he likes it.

The thirty-seven-year-old actor is, as he puts it, "a real Yankee"—born in New Hampshire, raised in Massachusetts, and educated in Maine and Connecticut. He discovered performing in a Bates College production of *Much Ado About Nothing,* then entered Yale Drama School in 1970. Oddly enough, he ended up graduating from Yale as a director, having switched majors after a pressure-packed first year in the acting department. Yet Robert Brustein, then the school's dean, predicted, "One day you're going to find out that you were born to be an actor."

It happened in 1975 with a play called *Yentl.* Shea, who'd been working as an assistant director at the Chelsea Westside Theater, was tapped for the role of Avigdor by his boss, Robert Kalfin.

"He was auditioning other actors," Kalfin recalls, "and I could see that he should just do the part himself. John has a wonderful sweetness and sincerity—he's not a phony in any way. It was weird, but I didn't even realize that he was good-looking until after I'd cast him. The human being was what I was responding to."

Shea, in turn, found himself responding to the challenge of the role. "Making that transformation into a yeshiva boy from Bechev, Poland, was like flying to the moon," he says. "I learned how to love to act." Topping it all off, the show became an Off-Broadway hit, later moving to Broadway.

"SHEA BRINGS A SENSE OF SELF-DISCOVERY TO THE ROLE, STARTING WITH HIS SELF-MOCKING PRIVATE EYE PERSONA, FINALEY EMERGING AS THE MAN OF AWARENESS AND CONSCIENCE."

—CLIVE BARNES,
New York Post

End of the World *(1984), Music Box Theatre, New York*

Copyright Laura Pettibone

With Tovah Feldshuh in Yentl *(1975), Eugene O'Neill Theater, New York*

"AS YENTL'S BAFFLED FRIEND, JOHN SHEA GIVES A REMARKABLY GRACEFUL, AFFECTING PERFORMANCE."

—HOWARD KISSEL,
Women's Wear Daily

After that, Shea worked steadily in both New York and regional theaters and picked up on-camera experience in TV films like *The Nativity* and *The Last Convertible.* Perhaps his most charming stage role was a lovesick fellow named Stephen Hurt ("as in pain") in the Public Theater's 1979 production of Peter Parnell's *Sorrows of*

"CONFRONTED WITH THE APPEALING MR. SHEA, A LEADING MAN WITH A KEEN SENSE OF COMEDY, IT IS DIFFICULT FOR WOMEN TO SAY NO, OR EVEN MAYBE."

—MEL GUSSOW,
The New York Times

With Pamela Reed in Sorrows of Stephen *(1979), Public Theater, New York*

Copyright © 1984 Martha Swope

Stephen. As producer Joseph Papp says, "John brings a mixture of seriousness and a kind of cavalier, casual way of performing. He's in the tradition of Cary Grant, which is very nice to see on the stage. He doesn't push."

Jill Clayburgh became so smitten with Shea's performance in *Stephen* that she asked him to play one of her lovers in *It's My Turn*. Alas, he says, the studio bigwigs didn't like the idea of Clayburgh sleeping with three different men, so his feature-film debut hit the cutting-room floor. "The only thing that's left of me in that movie is some roses I sent to her in a motel room," he says. "But it was actually a blessing."

"MR. SHEA IS A NEUROTIC OF THE FIRST RANK. HE'S ALTERNATELY SMUG, MERCURIAL, CRUEL, AND CHARMING."

—Frank Rich,
The New York Times

Copyright Laura Pettibone

American Days *(1981), Manhattan Theatre Club, New York*

A blessing indeed—*It's My Turn* sank, but two years later, *Missing* became a worldwide sensation. Shea had been offered the role of Charles Horman immediately after director Costa-Gavras saw his striking work as a record-company executive in the play *American Days* at the Off-Broadway Manhattan Theatre Club in January 1981. Though his part in *Missing* was small, Shea made it memorable. "Costa said, 'You'll be on the screen the same length of time that Yves Montand was in *Z*. When you're gone, everyone will miss you.' "

Courtesy of Universal Pictures

Missing *(1982)*

"CHARLES [IS] PLAYED WITH MODEST SIMPLICITY BY JOHN SHEA."

—VINCENT CANBY,
The New York Times

Two nights after the film's debut, *The Dining Room,* A. R. Gurney's gentle comedy of WASP manners, opened Off-Broadway. "It was an ensemble play, and I thought that would be good for my ego," Shea says. It was also an enormous hit, later filmed for public television, and John Shea felt his life change gears again.

Several notable projects followed. First: *Windy City,* a feature film about love and male friendship, which went unreleased for almost two years. The movie itself was deemed overly sentimental and disappeared soon after its release in the fall of 1984, but Shea came off as an appealing leading man. "It's not every day you get to say something about friendship and the nature of mortality," he says. "It was a story I wanted to tell."

His next role was Robert Kennedy in the seven-hour 1983 miniseries *Kennedy*. Before accepting the part Shea watched hours of documentary film footage at the Kennedy Library. When he heard Bobby Kennedy declare, "Only those who dare to fail greatly can ever hope to achieve greatly," he felt a personal challenge. Half a billion people around the world have since seen *Kennedy,* the largest audience for any dramatic film.

Following his work on *Kennedy,* Shea was tapped for the lead in *End of the World,* Arthur Kopit's satirical play about the arms race. Shea was cast as a playwright who begins investigating the government while doing research for a play about nuclear escalation. "I always perceived the role as a kind of Jimmy Stewart, all-American incorruptible family man," says director Harold Prince. "John was absolutely right for it."

"It was the hardest thing I've ever done, both emotionally and physically," says Shea, who was onstage throughout the evening, often addressing the audience directly. Though *End of the World*

"MR. SHEA . . . HAS PROVED TIME AND AGAIN THAT HE IS ONE OF OUR THEATER'S MOST SENSITIVE YOUNG ACTORS. HERE HE IS IN OUTSTANDING FORM."

—FRANK RICH,
The New York Times

Copyright © 1982 Susan Cook

With Ann McDonough and cast in The Dining Room *(1982), Playwrights Horizons, New York*

Kennedy *(NBC-TV, 1983)*

ran only a month, the actor was praised by critics for his handling of the play's serio-comic style.

After *Windy City*'s release, Shea left for England to play a storm trooper in the NBC-TV movie *Hitler's SS: Portrait in Evil.* His third feature film, a psychological thriller called *Honeymoon,* followed, marking the English acting debut of French star Nathalie Baye. "Going back and forth between theater and film helps stretch your talent," Shea says. "What you learn onstage, you can apply in the movies and vice versa. One form feeds the other."

"AS ROBERT KENNEDY, JOHN SHEA SUPPLIES AN UNEXPECTED BUBBLE OF ENERGY, A FIRE THAT MANY MAY NOT HAVE KNOWN HE PROVIDED IN THE KENNEDY WHITE HOUSE."

—LINDA STEVENS,
New York Post

In the coming years, Shea would like to tackle the great Shakespearean roles. "Romeo, Hamlet, Macbeth—those are the stepping stones in a true classical actor's career," he says. "When I'm an old man, I'll finish up with Lear and Prospero and call it a day."

"JOHN SHEA . . . IS THE CHIEF ATTRACTION IN *WINDY CITY*, A MOODY, REFLECTIVE LOOK AT A GANG OF HELL-RAISING BUDDIES FROM THE '60S, HOW THEY TURNED OUT 20 YEARS LATER, AND THE COMPROMISES THEY MADE ALONG THE WAY."

—REX REED,
New York Post

Copyright © 1984 CBS, Inc.

With Josh Mostel in Windy City *(1984)*

Meryl Streep

Meryl Streep is not only the most celebrated actor of her generation, but also one of the first who chose not to abandon the stage the moment she became a movie star. After making *The Deer Hunter,* she played Katharine in *The Taming of the Shrew* in Central Park. After winning an Oscar for *Kramer vs. Kramer,* she sang the role of Alice in Wonderland at the Public Theater. Though she hasn't appeared onstage since *Alice in Concert* in 1981, she still calls the theater her home.

Streep's rise to the peak of her profession has been swift and impressive, with very few missteps. She won her first standing ovation at age fifteen as Marian the librarian in *The Music Man* at Bernardsville High School, Bernardsville, New Jersey. Her work as Strindberg's Miss Julie made her the star of the college theater department at Vassar. After acting for a season with a traveling theater company in Vermont, she was awarded a scholarship to Yale Drama School in 1972.

At Yale, Streep again created a sensation, being cast in twelve to fifteen roles a year. One of her favorites was an eighty-year-old wheelchair-bound Russian translator in *The Idiots Karamazov,* a farce by classmates Christopher Durang and Albert Innaurato. "She was very, very funny," Durang says. "She's at her most exciting when she's playing someone who is not in any way like herself." Streep's teachers were already saying what every director since has said: "She can do anything."

Arriving in New York in the fall of 1975, Streep talked her way into an audition at the Public Theater and was immediately cast in *Trelawny of the Wells* alongside Mary Beth Hurt, Mandy Patinkin, and John Lithgow. She appeared in five more plays in the next nine months. Trite as it sounds, Meryl Streep had become an overnight success.

"THE PERFORMANCE OF THE SHOW COMES FROM MERYL STREEP AS HALLELUJAH LIL. SHE IS A KNOCKOUT. MAKING NO ATTEMPT TO IMITATE THE [LOTTE] LENYA GROWL, SHE SINGS AND ACTS WITH UTMOST SWEETNESS AND ENORMOUS STYLE."

—Clive Barnes, *The New York Times*

Happy End *(1977), Chelsea Theater Center, New York*

George E. Joseph

With John Lithgow in Trelawny of the Wells *(1975), Vivian Beaumont Theater, New York*

"GRACE AND CHARM [ARE] DISPLAYED BY MERYL STREEP AS A POISED AND VERY FUNNY IMOGEN PARROTT, THE FORMER WELLS ACTRESS WHO HAS ADVANCED TO A BETTER THEATER."

—DOUGLAS WATT,
New York *Daily News*

Copyright Van Williams

With Roy Poole in 27 Wagons Full of Cotton *(1976), Phoenix Theater Company, New York*

"MERYL STREEP IS SENSATIONALLY EFFECTIVE AS FLORA, THE SLOW-WITTED, PASSIONATE WIFE OF AN ELDERLY COTTON-GIN OWNER."

—BRENDAN GILL,
The New Yorker

Far from being pegged a pretty ingenue, Streep jumped from the drawing room of *Trelawny* to a front-porch swing as a fat Southern floozy in Tennessee Williams's *27 Wagons Full of Cotton*. Director Arvin Brown, who cast her after a reading, recalls that both of them had a few second thoughts during the first week of rehearsal. "The girl in this play is really a bovine creature, and after the first few days, it began to dawn on me how beautiful Meryl was," he says. "Then *she* came to me and said, 'I'm not sure I can play this.' That was an amazing thing for a young girl getting her big New York shot to do. 'But,' she said, 'I have one thing in mind.' The next day, she arrived wearing prosthetic breasts and rear padding and a Salvation Army housedress, and it was absolutely extraordinary. She suddenly *was* the character."

Copyright © Frederic Ohringer

With Paul Rudd in Henry V *(1976), Delacorte Theater, Central Park*

"WITH HER EXQUISITE HIGH-COMEDY TIMING, AND HER HAUGHTY, GUARDED, YET SUBTLY COQUETTISH WATCHFULNESS AS HENRY PURSUES HIS SOLDIERLY WOOING, SHE FINDS MORE IN THE PART THAN I HAD EVER KNOWN WAS THERE."

—JULIUS NOVICK,
The Village Voice

In performance, an artfully padded Streep clumped around the Phoenix Theater Company stage delivering lines like "You have to excuse me from thinking" through rubbery lips in an amusing Southern accent. The play shared a double bill with Arthur Miller's *A Memory of Two Mondays,* in which Streep played a brittle New York secretary. "People couldn't believe it was the same actress," Brown notes. Her versatility was rewarded with a Tony nomination.

After another role at the Phoenix, as the heroine of an 1895 melodrama called *Secret Service,* Streep was summoned by her mentor Joseph Papp to play two Shakespearean roles in Central Park: Princess Katharine in *Henry V* and Isabella in *Measure for Measure.* A month later, she was off to London to do her first film

George E. Joseph

"ESPECIALLY DELICIOUS IS MERYL STREEP'S HOUSEMAID DUNYASHA, ALL BORROWED GENTILITY AND SEXUAL FLUTTER."

—CHRISTOPHER PORTERFIELD, *Time*

With Raul Julia in The Cherry Orchard *(1977), Vivian Beaumont Theater, New York*

acting, a small part as Jane Fonda's bitchy friend in *Julia.*

Streep's breakneck pace continued through 1977. She stole the show as a flighty, fainting Dunyasha in Andrei Serban's staging of *The Cherry Orchard,* then made her Broadway debut in the Brecht-Weill musical *Happy End.* She played a virtuous German wife in the miniseries *Holocaust,* winning an Emmy Award for her performance. On the big screen, she brought depth and humanity to the part of Linda, the small-town girl torn between Christopher Walken and Robert De Niro in *The Deer Hunter.*

With Robert De Niro in The Deer Hunter *(1978)*

Courtesy of Universal Pictures

"MISS STREEP, WHO HAS LONG BEEN RECOGNIZED FOR HER FINE PERFORMANCES ON THE NEW YORK STAGE, GIVES A SMASHING FILM PERFORMANCE AS THE YOUNG WOMAN, WHO, BY TACIT AGREEMENT AMONG THE FRIENDS, BECOMES NICK'S GIRL BUT WHO STAYS AROUND LONG ENOUGH TO SUPPORT HERSELF."

—VINCENT CANBY, *The New York Times*

By Christmas 1978, when *The Deer Hunter* was released, Streep had done *The Taming of the Shrew* in Central Park and filmed three movie roles: an ambitious Southern lawyer in Alan Alda's *The Seduction of Joe Tynan,* Woody Allen's lesbian ex-wife in *Manhattan,* and, of course, the prodigal mother in *Kramer vs. Kramer.*

"IT'S EXCITING TO WATCH THE 29-YEAR-OLD STREEP TAKE MORE CHANCES THAN ANY OTHER YOUNG ACTRESS AROUND TODAY, CHARGING HER PERSONAL BEAUTY WITH AN EXPRESSIVE SPONTANEITY REMINISCENT OF THE YOUNG MARLON BRANDO."

—JACK KROLL, *Newsweek*

Copyright © 1984 Martha Swope

With Dixie Carter, Kathleen Quinlan, Elizabeth Wilson, and Colleen Dewhurst in Taken in Marriage *(1979), Public Theater, New York*

"THE CENTRAL FIGURE IS THAT OF THE MOVINGLY, ALMOST DANGEROUSLY MUDDLED MOTHER, PLAYED BY MISS STREEP IN WHAT IS ONE OF THE MAJOR PERFORMANCES OF THE YEAR. JOANNA IS NOT AN EASILY APPEALING CHARACTER. . . . THOUGH BEAUTIFUL, INTELLIGENT, WELL-EDUCATED, AND NO MORE THAN CASUALLY SELF-ASSERTIVE AT THE START, SHE GROWS INTO ONE OF THOSE FIERCELY DETERMINED PEOPLE WHO TALKS ABOUT FINDING HERSELF EVEN AS WE—AND SHE—SUSPECT THERE MAY BE NOTHING TO FIND BUT ANOTHER SET OF COMPROMISES."

—VINCENT CANBY, *The New York Times*

Robert Benton, director of *Kramer vs. Kramer,* remembers his first meeting with Streep, over breakfast with producer Stanley Jaffe and Dustin Hoffman. "I always thought it was the worst interview I ever had with an actor," he says, "with lots of long pauses, though she doesn't remember it that way. We talked for about twenty minutes, and as she walked to the door, I turned to Dustin and Dustin turned to me, and we said, 'That's Joanna Kramer.' And she was on target every inch of the way."

Copyright © 1981 Columbia Pictures Industries, Inc.

Kramer vs. Kramer *(1979)*

Streep won an Oscar for Best Supporting Actress for *Kramer* (she'd been nominated the year before for *The Deer Hunter*), along with Benton's grateful praise for rewriting her courtroom speech at the end of the movie. "There are some actors that you trust far above the line of duty," the director says, "and I have total trust in Meryl. She's extremely smart, very funny, and there are no limits to her talent."

After *Kramer,* Streep moved on to a trio of films that sent critics and journalists searching for fresh superlatives: *The French Lieutenant's Woman* (1981), *Sophie's Choice* (1982), and *Silkwood* (1983). Each performance earned an Oscar nomination, and Streep

"THERE IS ONLY ONE WONDER IN ELIZABETH SWADOS'S MUSICAL ADAPTATION OF LEWIS CARROLL, *ALICE IN CONCERT,* AND IT GOES BY THE NAME OF MERYL STREEP. DRESSED IN BLUE OVERALLS AND A WHITE TURTLENECK, MISS STREEP TRANSFORMS HERSELF INTO A DREAMY ALICE. . . . WHEN THE ACTRESS FALLS INTO THE RABBIT HOLE, SHE SEEMS TO TAKE LEAVE OF GRAVITY—EVEN THOUGH HER UNDULATING BODY NEVER ACTUALLY TAKES LEAVE OF THE FLOOR."

—Frank Rich,
The New York Times

With Mark-Linn Baker, Richard Cox, and Michael Jeter in Alice in Concert *(1981), Public Theater, New York*

Copyright © 1984 Martha Swope

"NOTHING IN HER EARLIER WORK FULLY ANTICIPATES *SOPHIE'S CHOICE*. MISS STREEP ACCOMPLISHES THE NEAR-IMPOSSIBLE, PRESENTING SOPHIE IN BELIEVABLY HUMAN TERMS WITHOUT LOSING THE SCALE OF MR. STYRON'S INVENTION. IN A ROLE OFFERING EVERY OPPORTUNITY FOR OVERSTATEMENT, SHE OFFERS A PERFORMANCE OF SUCH MEASURED INTENSITY THAT THE RESULTS ARE BY TURNS EXHILARATING AND HEARTBREAKING."

—Janet Maslin,
The New York Times

Courtesy of Universal Pictures

Sophie's Choice *(1982)*

was named Best Actress for her amazing characterization of the tragic concentration camp survivor Sophie Zawistowska.

The three films demonstrated her ability to assume different accents—English, Polish, Southern—with apparent ease, as well as her willingness to transform herself physically. Interestingly, her least successful movies have been contemporary stories requiring no special preparation. In *Still of the Night* (1982), her character lacked the tension and mystery necessary to sustain a Hitchcock-style thriller; in *Falling in Love* (1984), the flat dialogue did little to spark audience interest in her romance with Robert De Niro.

Copyright © 1981 Juniper Films; released by United Artists

The French Lieutenant's Woman *(1981)*

"ANY VIEWER FAMILIAR WITH THE NOVEL WILL BE TOUCHED . . . BY STREEP'S EERILY EXACT TRANSLATION OF FOWLES'S DESCRIPTIONS INTO SCREEN LIFE. . . . BUT THIS IS MORE THAN XEROXING EMOTIONS. IT IS THE CREATION OF A FILM CHARACTER THAT DOES PRECISE AND BREATHTAKING JUSTICE TO FOWLES, TO SARAH, AND THE ACTOR'S ART."

—RICHARD CORLISS,
Time

Streep continues to be offered movie parts other actresses would kill for, which is one reason she has been away from the theater for so long. In *Plenty,* for example, the 1985 film version of David Hare's hit play, she gets to show how an Englishwoman's work in the World War II underground deeply affects her psyche after the war.

"Making movies is hard work," Streep told *Esquire* on the occasion of being named to the magazine's 1984 list of outstanding young American achievers. "The theater is something I like better. And it's more welcoming to women. There's something about movies that I need, though. Making movies is sort of like exercise for my imagination. I turn slovenly very easily. I like the family kind of interaction that comes when you're working on a movie."

As producer of the film *Plenty,* Joseph Papp is understandably inclined to forgive Streep her absence from his stages. He predicts that she'll return to the theater in 1986 or 1987. Of his most illustrious protégée Papp says, "She's a superb technician with extraordinary resources who can play a great variety of roles in all media. And she's always learning. People have said it, and you might as well repeat it: She's one of the great actors of our time."

"MERYL STREEP, WITH THE HELP OF A MESSY, DARK BROWN HAIRDO, HAS SOMEHOW BEEN ABLE TO PLAY DOWN HER MOVIE STAR AURA SO THAT SHE ACTUALLY APPEARS TO BE A LIFE-SIZE, REMARKABLY AUTHENTIC EXAMPLE OF A WORKING CLASS WOMAN."

—KATHLEEN CARROLL,
New York *Daily News*

Copyright © Mary Ellen Mark

With Cher in Silkwood *(1983)*

Sigourney Weaver

Sigourney Weaver's comedic talent has helped her avoid the typecasting that might ordinarily go along with being a tall, gorgeous graduate of Yale Drama School. Long before she charmed Mel Gibson in *The Year of Living Dangerously,* Weaver was playing multiple roles onstage in Christopher Durang's crazy comedy *Titanic* and parodying Brecht and Weill in *Das Lusitania Songspiel,* a revue she and Durang wrote and performed together.

"Sigourney has a wonderful sense of humor that I'm longing for the movies to unleash further," says Durang, her friend since they attended Yale together. "As people have said about her, it's fun when a beautiful woman is willing to be silly. That silliness is very rare."

The daughter of Sylvester (Pat) Weaver, the NBC president who invented the *Today* and *Tonight* shows in the fifties, young Susan Weaver was raised on Manhattan's East Side and attended Ethel Walker, a girls' boarding school in Connecticut. At fourteen, she decided to take on a more dramatic first name, selecting "Sigourney" from a minor character in *The Great Gatsby.* She acted in school plays (often as men), but entered college at Stanford with the goal of becoming an English professor.

After four years of antiwar campus theater, plus more conventional roles in a troupe that toured the San Francisco area, Weaver was accepted into Yale. She found the work more structured and less irreverent than that at Stanford, although she did appear in an early Durang musical comedy in which she sang the title song, "Better Dead Than Sorry," while receiving shock treatments.

"Everyone talked about her because she was so striking," Durang recalls. "Also, she used to wear very eccentric clothing—I remember one odd outfit that had a sweatsuit top and a green

"FOR FLAT-OUT, FALLING-ON-THE-FLOOR LAUGHTER, NOTHING CAME CLOSE [DURING THE 1979–80 SEASON] TO *DAS LUSITANIA SONGSPIEL.* THIS LATE-NIGHT REVUE . . . MANAGED TO LAY WASTE TO ALMOST EVERY THEATRICAL HIT OF THE PAST TWO SEASONS. I'LL NEVER FORGET MR. DURANG, AS 'THE ELEPHANT MAN,' SINGING 'I LOVE NEW YORK,' OR MISS WEAVER DOING 'DIAMONDS ARE A GIRL'S BEST FRIEND' AS IT MIGHT HAVE BEEN WRITTEN BY BRECHT AND WEILL. . . . TONY AWARDS AND THEATER CRITICS MAY HAVE THEIR USES, BUT IT TAKES RUTHLESS SATIRISTS TO KEEP OUR CULTURE HONEST."

—Frank Rich,
The New York Times

With Christopher Durang in Das Lusitania Songspiel *(1980), Chelsea Theater Center, New York*

pajama bottom with tassels on it. We found that we had in common a sort of dark and quirky sense of humor."

Weaver didn't have an easy time of it when she arrived in New York, Yale degree in hand, in 1974. "It took me two years even to get a commercial," she says. "I went to a lot of open calls. Once, I walked in and the guy at the desk said, 'You're all wrong.' I said, 'This is for an attractive young woman,' and he said, 'No, you've got to have big breasts and be a show-girl type.' So I went home, put on a wig, stuffed my bra, and came back. I was ushered in

"MISS WEAVER . . . IS THE PRINCIPAL ATTRACTION IN *TITANIC*. SHE BEGINS IN PIGTAILS AND A TINY SKIRT AS A SEXY SHIRLEY TEMPLE AND ENDS AS A PREDATORY BLACK WIDOW IN DEEP DECOLLETAGE—A TRANSFORMATION SHE ACCOMPLISHES WITHOUT ONCE LOSING HER SENSE OF BALANCE."

—MEL GUSSOW,
The New York Times

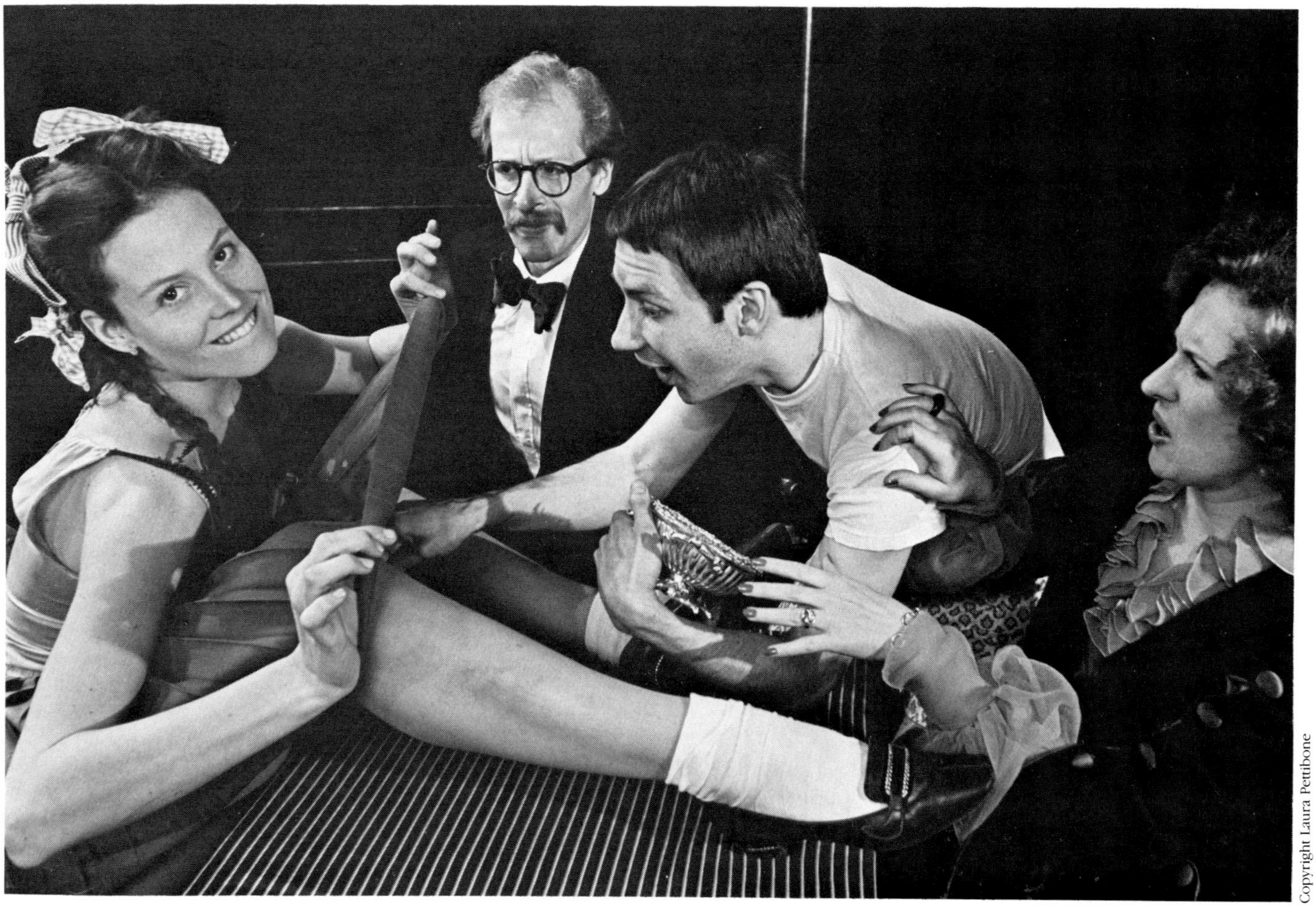

Copyright Laura Pettibone

With Stefan Hartman, Richard Peterson, and Kate McGregor-Stewart in Titanic *(1976), Vandam Theater, New York*

immediately and started to read, but I couldn't contain myself—I tore off the wig and said, 'You didn't even want to see me!' I was so shocked that casting people would type you the second you walked off the street instead of realizing that you're an actor and can transform yourself."

John Wulp

With Anne Jackson in Marco Polo Sings a Solo *(1977), Public Theater, New York*

Copyright © 1979 Twentieth Century-Fox Film Corporation

Alien *(1979)*

"THE CASTING ALL THE WAY IS IMPECCABLE . . . (MISS WEAVER IS ESPECIALLY GOOD.)"

—EDITH OLIVER, *The New Yorker*

"NEWCOMER SIGOURNEY WEAVER, A STRONG YOUNG ACTRESS WITH A TOUCH OF JANE FONDA, TAKES THE CLASSIC B-MOVIE WOMAN'S ROLE . . . AND RAISES IT TO A KIND OF ABSTRACT ENERGY AND AMBUSHED GRACE THAT'S LIKE WATCHING A BALLET OF PURE TERROR."

—JACK KROLL, *Newsweek*

She was finally hired as an understudy in Sir John Gielgud's 1975 Broadway production of *The Constant Wife.* "I rehearsed with him and he liked my work, which meant a lot," she says. "I hadn't been encouraged that much at Yale."

The following year, Weaver got an agent on the strength of her work aboard Durang's lunatic voyage on the *Titanic.* She played the captain's promiscuous pig-tailed daughter, then the lesbian lover of a passenger, then the angry daughter of that passenger. Though *she* received some good reviews, the production as a whole was savaged, with one critic wondering how the participants managed to earn MFAs from Yale.

As a curtain-raiser for *Titanic,* Durang and Weaver performed the first version of *Das Lusitania Songspiel.* Encouraged by the response, they revised and presented it again in 1980 with great success. Weaver calls the revue her favorite theatrical experience and says she hopes to do more cabaret work with Durang.

Copyright © 1984 Martha Swope

With Jim Borrelli, Kate McGregor-Stewart, and Stephen Collins in Beyond Therapy *(1981), Marymount Manhattan Theater, New York*

"AS THE HEROINE THERE IS SIGOURNEY WEAVER—JUST ABOUT THE BEST YOUNG ALL-PURPOSE ACTRESS IN TOWN. SHE GOES FROM ZANINESS THROUGH WHOLESOMENESS TO PATHOS WITH FAULTLESS ASSURANCE AND INGENUITY, IS A JOY TO HEAR AND BEHOLD."

—JOHN SIMON,
New York

Titanic led to a brief role in the soap opera *Somerset* ("There was too much emphasis on crying," she recalls), then another Yale classmate, Albert Innaurato, included Weaver in the original cast of *Gemini* (1976), his hit comedy about growing up Italian in Philadelphia. In 1977, Joseph Papp gave the actress her "first real paying job in the theater" alongside Joel Grey, Madeline Kahn, and Anne Jackson in John Guare's *Marco Polo Sings a Solo.* She played the wife of an astronaut who, via a thunderbolt, becomes pregnant with the first man of the twenty-first century.

"Sigourney has a quirkiness that contradicts her stature," Papp notes. "She's beautiful and commanding and yet she's 'cute'—she's basically very human. She really is a good comedienne."

Weaver's first three movies showed off more of the commanding side than the human, funny side. She became an international celebrity with *Alien* (1979), in which she played the bravest, smartest crew member aboard a spaceship under siege. In *Eyewitness* (1981), she was a TV reporter from an upper-class family who joins forces with a janitor (William Hurt) to solve a murder mystery. In *The Year of Living Dangerously* (1982), she was a British military attaché who falls in love with reporter Mel Gibson during the last days of the Sukarno regime in Indonesia.

While playing these ultra-cool movie heroines, Weaver kept her

"FOR WEAVER AND HURT, THE FILM IS A TRIUMPHANT DEMONSTRATION OF THEIR ECCENTRIC YIN-AND-YANG CHEMISTRY. HER SEXY PATRICIAN SPUNK SEEMS MADE TO BE MELTED BY HIS DOGGED ADORATION."

—DAVID ANSEN,
Newsweek

comedic gifts honed on the stage. She starred in the 1981 Off-Broadway premiere of Christopher Durang's *Beyond Therapy,* a stylized comedy about "relationships." In the summer of 1982, she

Copyright © 1983 MGM/UA Entertainment Co.

With Mel Gibson in The Year of Living Dangerously *(1983)*

"[DIRECTOR PETER] WEIR KNOWS WHAT'S SPECTACULAR ABOUT SIGOURNEY WEAVER: HER BRAINY FEMALE-HUNK PHYSICALITY—HER WIDE-AWAKE DARK EYES, THE PROTRUDING LOWER LIP, THE STRONG, ROUNDED, OUTTHRUST JAW, AND HER HANDS, SO LARGE THAT WHEN SHE EMBRACES GIBSON HER FIVE FINGERS ENCOMPASS HIS BACK. SHE USES HER FACE AND HER BODY, AND POURS ON THE PASSION AND LAUGHTER; SHE HAS THE KIND OF CAPACITY FOR ENJOYMENT THAT THE YOUNG SOPHIA LOREN HAD."

—PAULINE KAEL,
The New Yorker

Copyright Brigitte Lacombe/Liaison

With William Hurt in Eyewitness *(1981)*

teamed with John Shea for a revival of Philip Barry's *The Animal Kingdom* in Stockbridge, Massachusetts.

Her first movie comedy, *The Deal of the Century* (1983), turned out to be a critical and commercial disaster. Her second, *Ghostbusters,* became the most popular movie of 1984.

"I needed someone strong enough to give Bill Murray a run for his money," says director Ivan Reitman, who had seen Weaver only in *Alien* and *The Year of Living Dangerously.* "Sigourney was professional enough to actually audition and she just knocked me out." As Reitman points out, Weaver's character, a cellist, not only had to spar verbally with ghostbuster Murray, she also had to become possessed by evil forces. "Any good actor could play a possessed person, but I needed a possessed person who could also be funny. Sigourney has a quality of great strength that doesn't overwhelm her natural vulnerability."

While *Ghostbusters* was setting box-office records, David Rabe's *Hurlyburly* was becoming one of the biggest theatrical hits of 1984. Weaver played an earnest, spacey photographer who swapped psychobabble ("I got myself semi-straight—I was semi-functional anyway") with William Hurt. She stayed with the show for more than eight months, her first long run, and found that she adored it.

Copyright © 1984 Columbia Pictures Industries, Inc.

Ghostbusters *(1984)*

"MISS WEAVER LOOKS GREAT AND SHOWS HERSELF TO BE A WILLING COMEDIENNE AS WELL AS AN EXCELLENT FOIL FOR MR. MURRAY."

—JANET MASLIN,
The New York Times

Copyright © 1984 Martha Swope

With William Hurt in Hurlyburly *(1984), Promenade Theatre, New York*

"SIGOURNEY WEAVER PLAYS A TALL WOMAN WITH FILIGREE ADORABLENESS, AN EMOTIONAL CLICHÉ-MONGER WITH A SPRIG OF FRESH MINT IN EVERY PLATITUDE, AND BENIGHTEDNESS WITH CONSUMMATE INTELLIGENCE—THAN WHICH NO ONE COULD WANT MORE."

—JOHN SIMON,
New York

"I loved going to the theater eight times a week," she says. "It's such a nurturing place for the actor. There's something extremely satisfying about being able to continue working on a role. After the complications and chaos of doing a film, it's a relief simply to tell a story every night to a different group of people—you can forget about everything and let the story take you away."

Working on Broadway, another first, was a pleasant surprise as well. "I enjoyed the exhilaration of playing to that large a space," she says. "Whatever you did had to be fuller so it would be received by that many more people."

Her *Hurlyburly* experience made Weaver doubly eager to begin work on a movie—in French—with director Daniel Vigne and actor Gerard Depardieu in the spring of 1985. "I learned so much doing the play, and I'm anxious to let that knowledge come out in a film," she says. "The more I work onstage, the more I feel capable of doing movies. I'm so lucky that I'm able to go back and forth—I really think that's the perfect life for an actor."

Peter Weller

Onstage or on the screen, Peter Weller smolders. He creates characters with an attractive air of danger about them: a lonely trucker looking for love, a slick lawyer plotting his political future while his marriage crumbles, even a combination brain surgeon/scientist/rock singer who can drive a car through a mountain. His acting is sometimes frightening in its intensity, but he is always fascinating to watch.

An active member of the Actors Studio, Weller speaks of the importance of self-discovery in his performances. "Roles that are really demanding, about people who have problems that seem unsolvable, are fascinating to me because of the opportunity they give me to examine my own personal dilemmas," he says. "If you're a curious actor, you like big challenges that may make you uncomfortable."

Born in Stevens Point, Wisconsin, Weller spent his childhood on the move as the son of an army helicopter pilot. His original goal was to become a jazz trumpet player, and after his parents retired in Texas, he studied music at North Texas State University. Admitting to himself that he would never be a great musician, he relegated jazz to the status of a hobby and moved to New York to enter the American Academy of Dramatic Arts.

Even before his graduation in 1972, the twenty-five-year-old actor had made his Broadway debut, moving up from understudy to play the blind Vietnam veteran in David Rabe's *Sticks and Bones.* The show's producer, Joseph Papp, cast him in three other plays during the next several years, beginning in 1974 with *Macbeth*—or "the Scottish play," as Weller, who played Lenox, superstitiously calls it. "It was a production that was doomed not to open," he says, "starring Christopher Walken, John Heard, Stephen Collins, Christopher Lloyd, and Carol Kane. The whole

"IN WELLER'S ABSOLUTELY DAZZLING PERFORMANCE, [THE TRUCKER] STRUGGLES MANFULLY WITH ALL THE CONTRADICTIONS OF HIS COMPLEX PERSONALITY. WELLER LETS US SEE IN HIS FACE EXACTLY WHAT IS WHIRLING THROUGH THE MAN'S BRAIN: THE SENSITIVITY BEHIND THE MACHO SWAGGER, THE LONELINESS BENEATH THE GOOD-BUDDY JOKES, THE LONGING FOR LOVE AT THE ROOT OF IT ALL. IT IS AN INTENSELY FELT PERFORMANCE, CRAFTED IN AWESOME DETAIL AND DELIVERED WITH PERFECT CONTROL."

—Marilyn Stasio, *New York Post*

With Patricia Wettig in The Woolgatherer *(1980), Circle Repertory Company, New York*

George E. Joseph

With Mandy Patinkin in Rebel Women *(1976), Public Theater, New York*

"MANDY PATINKIN AND PETER WELLER PROVED IMPRESSIVE AS A COUPLE OF HOMOSEXUAL OFFICERS."

—CLIVE BARNES,
The New York Times

thing was horrible—Papp had us perform the entire twelve weeks in previews—but we had a great time."

Weller quit acting for eight months the following year because, he says, "I didn't know what my goals were." But in June 1976, playwright Thomas Babe lured him back by writing the role of a Union Army lieutenant for him in *Rebel Women,* a Civil War drama produced at the Public. Weller and Mandy Patinkin portrayed gay lovers and got better reviews than the play did.

Streamers, the last of David Rabe's Vietnam plays, followed, with Weller stepping into the role of the earnest midwestern recruit, Billy Wilson. "It was a phenomenal experience," Weller recalls. "Mike Nichols let the play reshape itself around me—he just let me go. That experience prepared me for everything else."

Joseph Papp, who produced *Streamers* at Lincoln Center's Mitzi Newhouse Theater, calls Weller "a very profound actor with a great deal of style. His sense of realism and truth is very strong. And he's deep—you always feel that he has much more than he delivers, and that's as it should be. You know that when the chips are down in his acting, he can let it come out."

Impressed with Weller's performance in *Streamers,* David

Mamet asked him to create the role of an emotionally repressed man opposite Patti LuPone in *The Woods*. The play's 1977 premiere, staged by Mamet in Chicago, received admiring reviews, but a 1982 New York revival was deemed dramatically unsatisfying by most critics.

"PETER WELLER IS PROPERLY HANDSOME AS THE YOUNG ROMANTIC PRETENDER, STEVE RUTLEDGE, A WRITER."

—ARCHER WINSTEN, *New York Post*

Copyright © 1984 Martha Swope

Streamers *(1976), Mitzi E. Newhouse Theater, New York*

Copyright © 1980 Warner Brothers Inc.

With Ali MacGraw in Just Tell Me What You Want *(1980)*

In the fall of 1977, Weller played an Orthodox Jew who becomes the head of a neo-Nazi party in an early episode of the *Lou Grant* TV series. Film director Richard Lester saw the performance and cast him as a bounty hunter in *Butch and Sundance: The Early Years* (1979). Director Sidney Lumet saw *that* and gave him the part of Ali MacGraw's boyfriend in the 1980 film comedy *Just Tell Me What You Want.*

Weller's return to the New York stage that summer, in William Mastrosimone's *The Woolgatherer,* was greeted with well-deserved critical acclaim. He gave a magnetic performance as a fast-talking truck driver who picks up a withdrawn young salesclerk at a five-and-dime. Swaggering around the tiny Circle Repertory Company stage, he filled the theater with a complex mix of humor, sexuality, and pathos.

Next came a memorable supporting role as Diane Keaton's lover in the 1982 film *Shoot the Moon.* The next year, Weller starred in a curious psychological thriller called *Of Unknown*

Copyright © 1981 Metro-Goldwyn-Mayer Film Co. and SLM Entertainment, Ltd.

With Diane Keaton in Shoot the Moon *(1982)*

"THE AWKWARD AND TENDER SEDUCTION SCENE BETWEEN WELLER AND KEATON IS A GREAT MOMENT."

—DAVID ANSEN, *Newsweek*

Copyright © 1982 Stephanie Saia

With Patti LuPone in The Woods *(1982), Second Stage, New York*

"WELLER COMMANDS OUR ATTENTION AT ALL TIMES. BUT *THE WOODS* IS UNREAL, NOT IN A FANCIFUL SENSE, BUT ON ITS OWN PSEUDO-REALISTIC TERMS."

—DOUGLAS WATT, New York *Daily News*

Origin. "It was about a guy who becomes obsessed with a domestic rat in his apartment," he explains. "It drives him insane." The movie was never released widely, but it prepared Weller for the two leading roles that were to follow.

In what is surely one of the funniest movies ever to have failed at the box office, Weller played the title character in *The Adventures of Buckaroo Banzai.* Described by critic Pauline Kael as "a kind of fermented parody of *M*A*S*H, Star Wars, Raiders of the Lost Ark,* and the TV series *The A-Team," Buckaroo* is about the exploits of a half-Japanese Renaissance man who invents a jet car that can pass through solid matter into the eighth dimension. His sidekicks, the Hong Kong Cavaliers, help him fight off evil Dr. Emilio Lizardo, played by John Lithgow.

Weller's wonderfully deadpan performance made lines like "Remember that no matter where you go, there you are" seem perfectly reasonable. He also sang and played his own rock compositions. Yet the film was released poorly, and appeared only

Copyright © 1984 Stephanie Saia

With Dianne Wiest in Serenading Louie (1984), Second Stage, New York

"MR. WELLER IS AS CHARISMATIC AS A WOULD-BE NEW FRONTIER POLITICIAN SHOULD BE—WHICH MAKES HIM ALL THE MORE PATHETIC ONCE HE DISCOVERS THAT THAT FRONTIER IS NOWHERE TO BE FOUND."

—Frank Rich,
The New York Times

briefly in New York almost two months after the good reviews appeared.

His part in the 1984 domestic drama *Firstborn* could hardly have been more different. Weller pulled no punches in playing a creepy drug dealer who moves in with single mother, Wendy (Teri Garr), and almost ruins her life. Only a truly frightening confrontation between him and her son brings Wendy to her senses. Weller liked the role because he felt it was the catalyst of the story, not another boyfriend on the sidelines.

Somehow, between each film, Weller found time to do a play. After *Of Unknown Origin,* he played Stanley Kowalski in *A Streetcar Named Desire* opposite Shirley Knight at the Hartman Theatre in Stamford, Connecticut, and after *Buckaroo Banzai,* he gave an intense performance as a hotshot lawyer with a crumbling marriage in Lanford Wilson's *Serenading Louie* at the Second Stage in New York.

"Theater overhauls the engine," he says, explaining his continuing willingness to work Off-Broadway for practically nothing. "The process of preparing in the theater is excruciating—you can't take a break or lay back. But it sure oils you up. When you're ready to do a movie, you're finely tuned."

Weller plans to produce his next film, the story, as he puts it, "of a man who has blown his life, and at the age of thirty-five grows up and redeems himself. I want to do plays and movies about people who learn something—or even, like *Firstborn,* about the fact that they *don't* learn anything."

"WELLER—HIS COBALT EYES BORROWED FROM PAUL NEWMAN, HIS IRON JAW FROM D.C. COMICS—MAKES A STALWART RENAISSANCE MAN FOR THE ATOMIC AGE."

—Richard Corliss, *Time*

Copyright Liaison

The Adventures of Buckaroo Banzai *(1984)*

JoBeth Williams

In a career that has included stage acting on and Off-Broadway and at half a dozen regional theaters, two soap operas, a pair of acclaimed TV movies, and feature films like *Poltergeist, The Big Chill,* and *American Dreamer,* JoBeth Williams has shown she can get to the heart of all kinds of characters.

"JoBeth has an absolute sense of truth and a wonderful imagination," says John Pasquin, who first directed her in 1974 in D. H. Lawrence's play *The Daughter in Law* (they were married eight years later). "She can make the most outrageously bizarre comic choices, as well as wonderful dramatic choices, and make them ring true emotionally. It's always something a little unusual, but it's always true."

The only child of a Houston opera tenor, Williams began acting in high-school plays, then headed north to Brown where she earned a degree in English in 1970. Her beauty and campus theater experience earned her a slot as one of *Glamour* magazine's top ten college girls of 1969–70.

"After graduation, I made the choice not to go to New York right away," Williams says. "Brown wasn't a theater school, and I knew I needed training. I auditioned for Adrian Hall at Trinity Square Repertory Company in Providence and was lucky enough to be accepted."

"We were just beginning a classical rep company," Hall recalls, "and I was recruiting attractive young performers from around the country. JoBeth was a natural—beautiful, well educated, and she had a great respect for what we were doing. She did small roles at first, but I began to pay attention to her when she shaved her eyebrows to play one of the whores in *Threepenny Opera.* She was sensational."

Williams spent two and a half years at Trinity Square and

"THE MYSTERIOUSLY BEAUTIFUL JoBETH WILLIAMS IS PERFECT AS LYDIE. MISS WILLIAMS HERE COMES INTO HER OWN AS AN ACTRESS OF COMPELLING COMPLEXITY—HER SLITHERS IN THE MOVING SANDS OF PASSION AND IDEALISM ARE CONVEYED WITH A PIQUANT MIXTURE OF QUICKSILVER AND SERENITY."

—CLIVE BARNES,
The New York Post

With James Woods in Gardenia *(1982), Manhattan Theatre Club, New York*

William L. Smith

With James Eichelberger, Robert Black, and Tom Mason in Son of Man and the Family *(1971), Trinity Square Repertory Company, Providence, Rhode Island*

Copyright © 1985 Cliff Moore

With Anthony McKay in The Daughter in Law *(1974), McCarter Theater, Princeton, New Jersey*

played six roles, including Oscar Wilde's wife in a drama called *Feasting with Panthers,* which became an acclaimed PBS-TV film in 1974. Her first play away from Trinity Square was *The Daughter in Law* at Princeton's McCarter Theater, followed by Michael Weller's *Moonchildren* in Boston and later Off-Broadway, again under the direction of John Pasquin.

After Williams settled in New York, she combined regional theater work in Williamstown, Massachusetts, Washington, D.C., and Philadelphia with leading roles in the soap operas *Somerset* (1975–76) and *The Guiding Light* (1977). "I thought that soaps would be a good way to learn about working with cameras," she says, "and I did find it helpful—it teaches you to work quickly and to adapt to changing circumstances. But I didn't stay very long in either show because I found myself getting stir crazy playing the same part day after day."

"MISS WILLIAMS, A NEW YORKER MAKING HER DEBUT AT McCARTER, IS A HIGHLY SKILLED, SPARKLING ACTRESS WHOSE PLAINTIVE STARES AND SHARP WORDS RING TRUE. THE BEST TIMES OF THE NIGHT ARE HER SCENES WITH McKAY, IN WHICH THE REPRESSED HELL-FIRE OF MINNIE FEEDS ON THE INFURIATING SULLENNESS OF LUTHER—A HIGHLY COMBUSTIBLE FUEL."

—ANDREW LANTNER,
Trenton Evening Times

Williams's first film performance was brief but oh-so-memorable: a nude encounter with Dustin Hoffman's young son in *Kramer vs. Kramer* (1979). "We wanted an actress who was a consummate comedian and could really hold her own against Dustin," says director Robert Benton. "In interviews, we looked to see which ones he couldn't push around, and JoBeth was extraordinary about that. Her work in the film was wonderful, but it was unfortunately necessary to cut her part down because we found that people only wanted to see Ted Kramer and his son."

Nevertheless, her acting in *Kramer* led to roles as Gene Wilder's girlfriend in *Stir Crazy* (1980) and Christopher Walken's ex-wife in *The Dogs of War* (1981). Again, in *Dogs of War,* her part was slashed, but again, it didn't matter: Steven Spielberg saw a longer version of the film in London and was so impressed with Williams that he asked her to star in *Poltergeist* (1982). The actress

Copyright © 1983 Columbia Pictures Industries, Inc.

Kramer vs. Kramer *(1979)*

"[JoBETH WILLIAMS'S] WORK CONVINCES US TO ACCEPT THE SUPERNATURAL EVENTS EVEN AS WE HOOT AT THEM. MISS WILLIAMS'S MOTHER IS A SWINGING, FUNNY AMERICAN MOM WHO, WHEN THE CHIPS ARE DOWN, DOESN'T HESITATE TO EMBARK ON A JOURNEY TO HELL TO RETRIEVE A LOST CHILD. THE ROLE IS WELL WRITTEN AND EXCEEDINGLY WELL PLAYED."

—VINCENT CANBY, *The New York Times*

Copyright © 1982 Metro-Goldwyn-Mayer Film Co. and SLM Entertainment, Ltd.

With Craig T. Nelson and Oliver Robins in Poltergeist *(1982)*

added a refreshing note of humor and compassion to an otherwise terrifying tale of a child being held hostage by ghostly forces within the family's own home.

Meanwhile, Williams was continuing to work on the New York stage. She won good personal notices in the Broadway flop *Ladyhouse Blues* (1979) and played a repressed Westchester housewife in the Off-Broadway hit *A Coupla White Chicks Sitting Around Talking* (1981). She then created the role of Lydie Breeze in John Guare's post–Civil War drama *Gardenia* (1982) at the Manhattan Theatre Club.

"Films are very exciting," says Williams, "but for an actor, I think theater is more rewarding. You get to go from point *A* to point *Z* every night, to experience the entire arc of the character. There's a certain emotional catharsis in doing that. In a film, shooting piecemeal, it takes enormous concentration to hold on to where you are with the character. That can be tricky for some film actors who have never done theater. You can hit it in one take and not be able to find it again."

"JOBETH WILLIAMS CAN SAY MORE BY DIRECTING HER BIG SAD EYES OFF-SCREEN THAN VOLUMES OF EMILY DICKINSON."

—RICHARD CORLISS, *Time*

After *Poltergeist,* Williams found herself in demand for film and TV projects. She played a Colorado sheriff in Alan Rudolph's quirky thriller *Endangered Species* (1982), then the housewife Karen in Lawrence Kasdan's *The Big Chill* (1983). "I begged Larry to consider me for the lawyer," she says, "because that was a role I really responded to—a career woman who was trying to make the decision about having a baby. The suburban housewife was not something that I identified with at all. And he said, 'No, I want you to play this role because I believe you'll bring another dimension to it.' " She did.

On television, Williams starred in two of the most talked about movies of 1983: ABC's nuclear holocaust drama *The Day After* and *Adam,* NBC's heartbreaking saga of the search for a missing child. She received an Emmy nomination for *Adam* plus the satisfaction of helping reunite parents with a dozen of the missing children pictured at the end of the broadcast.

Teachers, a popular 1984 comedy, included JoBeth Williams's second nude scene, in which she briefly shed her clothes in the school hallway in an attempt to bring a formerly idealistic teacher (Nick Nolte) to his senses. She next starred in the romantic comedy *American Dreamer* as a housewife who wins a trip to Paris, gets hit by a car, and wakes up believing she's the leading character in her favorite romance novels. Williams and Tom Conti, as the real novelist's son, made an attractive pair and shared some

With Kevin Kline, William Hurt, and Glenn Close in The Big Chill *(1983)*

Copyright Jean Pierre Bonnot/Gamma-Liaison

With Tom Conti in American Dreamer *(1984)*

"WILLOWY JOBETH WILLIAMS SEEMS TO BE HAVING A TERRIFIC TIME AS REBECCA, AND SHE'S GENEROUS WITH IT; SHE'S SO VIGOROUSLY OBLIVIOUS THAT THE SIGHT GAGS SPIN MERRILY OFF HER."

—DAVID EDELSTEIN,
The Village Voice

funny moments, but most critics felt the movie seemed too much like a fifties sitcom.

"I was sad that *American Dreamer* wasn't better received, because for me it was such a breakthrough to play a strong comedic heroine," Williams says. "The old adage about comedy being harder than dying is true in many ways. In *White Chicks,* for example, we knew every night if something was working, by the audience response. When you're in front of a camera, it's very cold, and the crew can't laugh out loud. But I loved doing an out-and-out boffo comedy, and I hope to do more of it."

In the fall of 1984, Williams co-starred with Jon Voight in *Desert Bloom,* a feature film about nuclear testing in Nevada during the fifties. "As all actors do, Jon and I were talking on the set about all the plays we'd like to do together," she says. "The vicissitudes of this business are so strong that you almost feel you have to take good movie scripts when they're offered. But there's no thrill in the world like doing a play before a live audience. No amount of 'stardom' in film can supplant that immediate rush of having an audience respond to you. If you're serious about theater, you need to go back to it."

Treat Williams

No one can accuse Treat Williams of dodging a challenge. He was twenty-eight years old when he began filming the demanding title role in *Prince of the City,* Sidney Lumet's three-hour drama about police corruption in New York. A year later, he took on the formidable task of replacing Tony Award–winner Kevin Kline in Broadway's *The Pirates of Penzance.* In 1984, he accepted the even more intimidating job of wrestling the ghost of Marlon Brando in *A Streetcar Named Desire* on network TV.

"You have to give him a lot of credit," says *Pirates* producer Joseph Papp. "I watched him prepare when he took over Kevin's job. It was not his style at all and yet he made it work for him. He's serious about his work."

"His strength as an actor is his courage," adds John Ferraro, who directed Williams in *Pirates* and the 1982 Off-Broadway play *Some Men Need Help.* "Treat doesn't think, 'Here I am following Kevin Kline.' He just says, 'Okay, here's how *I'm* going to do the Pirate King.' He's a remarkable talent."

For Williams, *Pirates* and *Streetcar* were cases of accepting the best roles available to him. "I figure you're going to be compared to other actors all your life," he says. "I try to keep my thinking on a higher plane."

Treat (an ancestor with the same name signed the Declaration of Independence) got a quick start in the theater after graduating from Franklin and Marshall College as a drama major in 1973. He found an agent with the help of childhood friend Judy Abbott (daughter of George) and, within a week, became John Travolta's understudy in *Grease.* Featured roles in *Over Here,* a musical with the Andrews Sisters, and a revival of *Bus Stop* followed, along with tiny parts in the movies *The Ritz, The Deadly Game,* and *The Eagle*

"TREAT WILLIAMS HAS STYLE AS A HOLLYWOOD GO-GETTER."

—CLIVE BARNES, *New York Post*

With Deborah May in Once in a Lifetime *(1978), Circle in the Square Theatre, New York*

Gary Wheeler/Equity Library Theatre

With Darlene Parks in Bus Stop *(1975), Equity Library Theatre, New York*

"AS BO, TREAT WILLIAMS PRODUCED THE PROPER MIXTURE OF JUVENILE BOISTEROUSNESS AND SULKY CONTRITION."

—LAWRENCE VAN GELDER, *The New York Times*

Has Landed. Williams also returned to *Grease* as head greaser Danny Zuko for several months in 1976.

Before long a pair of highly appealing roles were offered to him: the romantic lead in a hilarious revival of Kaufman and Hart's *Once in a Lifetime* (1978), and Berger, the hippie leader in the film version of *Hair* (1979). "I loved that guy," Williams says of Berger, and who wouldn't? He got to crash—literally—a stuffy debutante party and dance up and down Manhattan singing at the top of his lungs.

Billy Rose Theatre Collection, New York Public Library at Lincoln Center

With Robin Lamont in Grease *(1976), Royale Theatre, New York*

Copyright © 1979 CIP Film Produktions GMBH; released by United Artists

Hair *(1979)*

"A ROLLICKING MUSICAL MEMOIR . . . THE ENTIRE CAST IS SUPERB, ESPECIALLY TREAT WILLIAMS AS BERGER, THE HIPPIE LEADER."

—VINCENT CANBY,
The New York Times

The young actor's charm and energy led Sidney Lumet to hire him for *Prince of the City,* a movie that could hardly be more different from *Hair.* In preparing to play an Italian narcotics detective, Williams spent a month roaming around New York with street cops and talked at length with Robert Leuci, the real-life counterpart for his character.

Lumet had no doubt that Williams could handle the subtleties of the role. "Treat has great power but also an innate sweetness and naïveté," he says. That sentiment is echoed by Joseph Papp: "He's tough and boyish at the same time and has a vulnerable quality that's very engaging. He just lays it right out there, and you believe him."

Williams has experienced the ups and downs of celebrity more than most young actors of his caliber. After the acclaim of *Hair,* his next two movies (*Why Would I Lie?* and *1941*) were flops. And after *Prince of the City* and a *Newsweek* cover with William Hurt and Elizabeth McGovern, his feature-film career slowed again. "Everything is cyclical," he says. "You have periods when parts are coming your way and you have quieter periods. At the time of *Prince of the City* and *Pirates,* my life was not my own. I decided then that when things got quiet, I would enjoy it."

"TREAT WILLIAMS COMBINES BRAZEN COCKINESS AND VULNERABILITY. . . . HIS DANNY IS A TOUGH ITALIAN KID, BUT HE'S ALSO EXCITABLE, SWEATY, NERVOUS . . . WHEN THE PROSECUTORS FORCE [HIM] INTO TESTIFYING AGAINST HIS BUDDIES, WILLIAMS'S AGONY LEAVES YOU EXHAUSTED AND SHAKEN."

—David Denby, *New York*

Prince of the City *(1981)*

Copyright © Barbra Walz/Outline

"TREAT WILLIAMS IS BUOYANTLY FUNNY AS THE NEW PIRATE KING."

—DOUGLAS WATT,
New York *Daily News*

Copyright © 1984 Martha Swope

The Pirates of Penzance *(1981), Uris Theatre, New York*

Not that Williams has been idle. He took particular pride in *Some Men Need Help,* John Ford Noonan's two-character Off-Broadway comedy-drama in which he played a WASPy young alcoholic. "It's a very unsympathetic role in the first act," says director John Ferraro, "and I wanted someone the audience would care about automatically. Treat has a great deal of charm, but he didn't try to use that. He went all out, and it was very powerful."

On television, Williams starred as Jack Dempsey in a 1983 CBS biographical movie, in addition to his role as Stanley Kowalski in *Streetcar* on ABC. On film, he played a union boss in Sergio Leone's epic *Once Upon a Time in America* and co-starred with Kris Kristofferson in the action thriller *Flashpoint,* both of which were released in 1984.

"Treat gives a different kind of performance onstage and on

film," notes Ferraro. "The film frame is a little proscenium, and he knows how to use that; the stage is another kind of proscenium, and he knows how to use that, too. He knows what the theater's about and is extremely versatile."

Copyright © 1984 Martha Swope

With Philip Bosco in Some Men Need Help *(1982), 47th Street Theater, New York*

"MR. WILLIAMS IS QUIETLY EFFECTIVE EXPLAINING THAT HE REALLY DROVE HIS WIFE AWAY BECAUSE SHE WAS WILLING TO TAKE HIM AS HE WAS, WHEREAS HE COULDN'T STAND BEING THE SECOND-RATER THAT HE IS."

—WALTER KERR,
The New York Times

Copyright © Nancy Ellison/Sygma

With Ann-Margret in A Streetcar Named Desire *(ABC-TV, 1984)*

"AS STANLEY, TREAT WILLIAMS EPITOMIZES 'BRUTAL DESIRE' AND 'ANIMAL FORCE' EVERY BIT AS MUCH AS BRANDO DID."

—JOHN LEONARD, *New York*

Reflecting on his choice of roles, Williams sees himself moving away from "dark, complicated" characters like the detective in *Prince of the City* toward "more normal, straightforward human beings." One of them was the New York lawyer in *Scandal,* Michael Bennett's proposed follow-up to the smash Broadway musical *Dreamgirls.* Beginning in the fall of 1984, Williams devoted nine months to the workshop development of the show, though, in the end, Bennett chose not to bring it to Broadway in the spring of 1985. "I loved getting up and going to work," Williams says. "Michael, of course, has an incredible knowledge of the theater, and everything was very collaborative." He adds, quite understandably, "It was really great to be doing my own part."

Index

Also available from Quill

My Heart Belongs
Mary Martin

The autobiography of one of America's most beloved stars.
0-688-03652-X

The Steven Spielberg Story
Tony Crawley

Looks behind the legend of the *wunderkind* director who has brought us *Jaws, Raiders of the Lost Ark,* and *E.T.* With photos.
0-688-02510-2

Hollywood Color Portraits
John Kobal

Dietrich, Gable, Hayworth, Bogart, Garbo, Presley, Monroe . . . These are but a handful of the stars featured in this dazzling collection of full-page color portraits.
0-688-04821-8

Unforgettable Hollywood
Nat Dallinger

A delightful collection of nearly 250 of the best of Nat Dallinger; including all the greats, captured in charming informality.
0-688-02475-0

AVAILABLE AT YOUR LOCAL BOOKSTORE